Under Sail

SOUTH DEVON

and

DARTMOOR

Raymond B Cattell

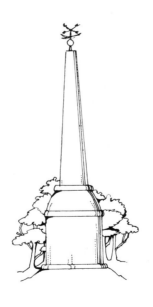

OBELISK PUBLICATIONS

OTHER BOOK IN THIS SERIES
Adventure Through Red Devon by Raymond B Cattell

PLATE ACKNOWLEDGEMENTS
Jane Reynolds for all drawings
R W Norton for pages 4, 6, 39, 46, 50 and 55
Chips Barber for pages 20, 21, 34,38, 64 and 140
Dr Malim for page 51
Chapman & Son, Dawlish for page 53

Cover photograph - a distant view of Haytor, by R W Norton
Back cover - the curving coastline towards Bigbury, by Chips

All other illustrations are taken from the original book
"Under Sail Through Red Devon" published by Maclehose in
1937

Published by Obelisk Publications, 2 Church Hill, Pinhoe,
Exeter. This edition was redesigned, refitted and relaunched
by Sally Barber.

Printed in Great Britain by Short Run Press, Sowton, Exeter

ISBN 0 946651 06 X

CONTENTS

INTRODUCTION

"Under Sail Through South Devon and Dartmoor" may seem an unusual title for a book - sailing through Dartmoor? But the explanation is simple. In the summers between 1931 —- 1935 Ray Cattell made a series of voyages along the coast of Devon and up many of the rivers. Often, when the paddling became too wearisome or the rivers too shallow, he and his various partners set off to explore the innermost parts of Devon, the rugged heights of Dartmoor and various other hill ranges.

When the book was originally published it bore the title "Under Sail Through Red Devon" - the 'Red' relating to the richly coloured soils and cliffs so predominant in South and East Devon. The original book was a much bulkier edition so re-publication was thought desirable in two halves. The first half has now appeared as "Adventure Through Red Devon" and covers the area between Paignton and Lyme Regis and includes voyages up the Exe and Teign. This book completes the story, a timeless adventure of youthful wanderings against a backcloth of wonderful scenery and colourful characters. Inevitably many of the places Ray visited have changed, some for the better, many for the worse. However the landscape remains largely the same.

I have read this story many, many times and I never tire of reading it. It is a wonderful book which I hope will give you as much pleasure as it has given me!

Chips Barber

Chapter 1

Beyond Berry Head

The Calendar definitely said it was Autumn and Mr. Pelosi, in obedience to its dictates, had wrought the annual miracle of converting his ice cream cart (standing by the Pier) into a fish and chip van (standing by Paignton Station). But the weather clerk had himself gone on holiday or perchance had fallen asleep in the heat, for summer weather continued and the shores were still clothed in the most luscious green.

An expert, maybe, would have noted an undue calmness in the briefer days, a little milky mist clinging to the valleys in the mornings, a bracing touch in the dawn breeze and a grey glitter in the waves it shepherded along. For some reason books on weather lore always insist that the most important weather signs are only to be observed at sunrise. To this unearthly hour they attach the superstitious importance which the ancient oracles attached to the liver of a piebald goat. Consequently, less fanatical people like myself, who cannot be guaranteed to observe anything but breakfast before ten o'clock in the morning, are unjustly barred from the profession of weather prophet.

To me these days of early autumn in South Devon, and particularly in Torbay, are always an unmitigated delight. Quite suddenly the visitors' ranks begin to thin out, the tents and the flags go down. One beholds the straggling remnants of a decimated army of invaders.

Gazing on the forlorn rout of these barbarians, in full retreat to office and workshop, one cannot help feeling a sympathetic melancholy. I know there are people for whom the spectacle of others going to work is unalloyed joy, but since I would rather work ten hours a day in Devonshire than six anywhere else, my relief at the rebirth of the real Torbay is tinged by 'Weltschmerz' at the thought of what these others are missing. Yet I am well informed that this sympathy is wasted; that the barbarians vastly prefer their snug and smug winter city life to all the wind that blows over the moors and sea. Whatever conflicts occur are swamped in the delight of seeing Torbay emerge again. Beach inspectors and other curious birds migrate, presumably to do their fell work on tropical shores. An early storm washes the beaches sweet and clear of papers, deck chairs and other rubbish: the crowded and noisy motor-boat gives way to smooth-sailing fishing craft: the froth of advertisement subsides; spaciousness comes back like a queen.

We spread ourselves in Paradise Regained, dropping into the old picnic haunts by Elbury Cove, singing our way home across the still waters in the purple twilight. Alas, the cancer of brick and mortar has spread even over the little cliffs beyond Goodrington. At Elbury itself, fortunately, the land has fallen into the hands of people who can plan, who employ artists - Staverton Builders, who hail from that Dartington Hall which we shall meet anon. The winding road and simple white houses provide a pleasing spectacle vastly different from conglomerate Paignton, yet still perhaps not so attractive as the flag and marigold-strewn marshes which used to delight the eye between Churston Woods and the hills.

Spoilt or not, the bay will always hold my affection for the reason of boyhood memories. By Roundham Head we had amused ourselves mightily as boys by making a highly-coloured chart of all the rocks, channels and currents, embellished with such names as Bloody Channel, Dead Man's Rock and Hell's Deep. As it was war time all channels of importance had to be mined with

lemonade bottles filled with gunpowder. Fortunately for
the nerves of local fishermen our crude detonating
devices never functioned. Our fleet of three - a
dinghy, the *Dolphin* and a canoe of canvas - would often
be seen anchored below the concrete fortress which we

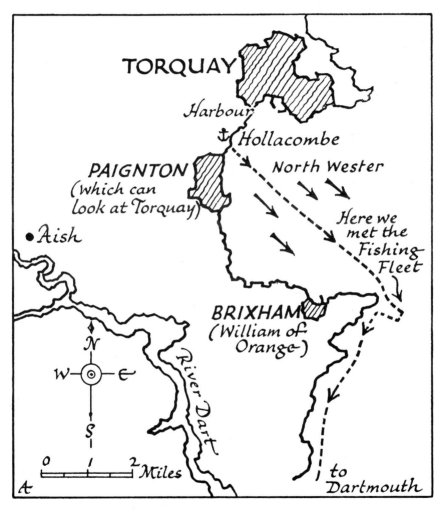

built in an eerie in the highest part of the cliff. We
were very proud of that fortress for every bucket of
cement, sand and water used in its construction had to
be toilsomely carried up a ladder of doubtful footholds

from the sea edge, and many a bucket fell from aching fingers just when the recipient at the top was leaning over to take it. A soulless town council has now blasted away both the fortress and the cliff on which it stood - to make ordered 'pleasure grounds' for children and adults. And even though it has been well done I am reluctant to believe that before this we, as children, did not know what pleasure was.

It was a history lesson which ultimately brought us into disgrace. We were told of the "strong and mighty chain" stretched across the entrance of the Dart to keep out pirates. On the following evening, after a losing battle with an opposing fleet of fishermen's children, in unauthorised possession of their fathers' dinghies, we retreated by a short cut over Bloody Reef into Paignton Harbour. After mining the entrance with three lemonade bottles we remembered Dartmouth, and, borrowing a wire hawser which had for some time lain on the quayside, we stretched it tightly across the harbour mouth.

It was unfortunate that a naval supply boat came into harbour before our pursuers arrived. The coxswain, poised in that debonair manner and wearing that condescending expression peculiar to naval men when entering third-rate harbours, was very nearly cut off in his prime by the unseen hawsers. What he said to the harbour master and what the sorely-tried harbour master said to us escapes my memory now - I only know that for repeating one of the least objectionable of their poetic fancies in school, next day, we had five hundred lines apiece.

With such cheerful associations we found it hard to leave Torbay; but this incredible summer couldn't last for ever and I wanted to get *Sandpiper* around Berry Head and up the Dart to Dartington, where our cottage was being furnished, before the equinoctial gales began.

By road it is only seven miles over the hills to Dartington, but by reason of the peculiar formation of the land, the peninsula of Berry Head and Kingswear, and the sinuous curving of the Dart, it makes a good sea trip of twenty-seven miles. The first mate, having to prepare the Dartington cottage for a 'house warming' party that night, again refused to come aboard, but instead issued strict orders that I was to get to Dartington in time to change into a boiled shirt by seven o'clock. That gave something of a record-breaking character to the voyage. Fortunately the conditions were excellent; a north-west wind to blow me out of the bay and a tide which turned at Dartmouth at one o'clock promised to carry me far up the river. Everything depended on not missing the tide connection at Dartmouth.

Sandpiper set off with lovely motion before the north-wester and for a time I headed straight for the edge of the austere ramparts of Berry Head which, from my low position, loomed like a great battleship across the southern horizon. Soon I was reminded by the bounding movement that the 'fetch' of a strong north-wester across four miles of water would raise such a sea as would make it unwise to hold straight on. Discretion indicated the longer way around by clinging to the coast. But next moment I thought of being ignominiously late for the party, and held straight on. Normally I look upon a trip to Berry Head and back as an afternoon's sail. To-day I was under its cliffs in twenty minutes, with Sandpiper plunging though the waves like a hungry porpoise in spite of my kicking the rudder from side to side to check her yawing. In a moment I was becalmed under the shadow of the headland and there a curious current seized me (there is always a tide race round Berry Head) and whisked me straight out to sea, eastwards, with astonishing speed, until Berry Head began to look quite small again. With that I picked up some more wind.

Here I met the brown-sailed Brixham fishing fleet, standing in from sea, heavily-laden. The first three trawlers were as dead in line as cruisers at a Royal Review and were bearing straight down upon me. I debated whether I might construe the navigation rules to mean that they must give way to my cockleshell. True, they were close hauled on the starboard tack (to which port gives way) but I also was fairly close hauled on the same tack and might come under the heading of "ship overtaken" which must be avoided by those overtaking. I held straight on.

A large and jovial face appeared over the bulwarks of the first boat - eyes somewhat bulbous with astonishment as they surveyed *Sandpiper*.

"Where be gwain tu in ee?"

"Dartmouth," I shouted.

This evidently struck him as a very ripe joke and his laughter brought a second surprised face to the side.

"Tes gwain to blaw up a bit zoon. You'd bedder git in under," he remarked, in a more concerned tone, nodding to the cliffs.

To avoid argument I edged a point nearer to the cliffs, proceeding almost parallel to the trawlers.

"What sort of a catch this time?" I asked.

"Just a tidy l'il haul, baint as good as twas you knaw."

For once I knew that a grumbling fisherman was speaking the truth. The famed Brixham fishing fleet had dwindled sadly since the war. During the war itself it suffered heavy loses when a German U-boat popped up in the middle of the becalmed vessels and shelled every boat until it foundered. But since the war, owing to the enormous number of wrecks which now litter the floor of the Channel, from beyond the Start to Portland, the trawling gear is so often caught and destroyed that the fishermen are getting tired of their losses, losses which no skill can avoid, and are selling their boats to those who make yachts out of them. And fine deep sea cruising yachts they make, incidentally.

Meanwhile the hardiest carry on, hoping that the Admiralty will one day set the Navy to blow up those hideous skeletons on the floor of our English Channel.

In a while I waved good-bye to my big brown friends.

"Mind the fishes doan't eat 'ee," was the skipper's parting shot.

I watched them sail into Brixham - dear old unchanging Brixham - "the haven under the hill"; home of the sturdiest and most spirited sons of Devon. Alike in the freshness of morning or when the chimney smoke gathers over the harbour valley in the coloured twilight, you will find the simple grey houses and the homely folk of Brixham a spectacle satisfying to the eye and to the heart.

Here, with these men, whose days are closely packed with adventure, toil, enterprise and disaster, with life and death, worked the Reverend Francis Lyte, Vicar of Brixham for twenty-five years. Towards the end of his days he prayed that he might be allowed to write some poem to crown his life work. On one of his last evenings in Brixham he climbed up to Berry Head as the sun was setting and wrote the immortal hymn, "Abide with me".

To pass around Berry Head is to find oneself in a new world. A door shuts upon the friendly garden of Torbay and one finds oneself in the draughty expanses of the Channel, cold-shouldered by high ramparts of cliffs, rugged and unscalable. In Brixham people say of a very old person in failing health "He's going round the Head" just as the Greeks would talk of "crossing the Styx", and if you sail round the Head you will realise the aptness of the reference to another world.

Stiff squalls of wind now blew off the land whenever I came opposite a valley, ruffling the sunlit water into a profound indigo blue against which the white cliffs stood out in dazzling fairness. This stretch from Berry Head to Dartmouth is a panorama of virgin loveliness. No easy roads run to the coast, and the high rugged cliffs have not proved attractive to the builder.

First we sight the little white coastguard station keeping its lonely vigil in the Mansands valley. Here in the last years of the war I used to strut up and down with a telescope under the arm of my sea-scout jersey - a terror to the U-boats of those parts. Somehow, in spite of my vigilance, they managed, to my surprise, to sink a boat nearly every week between Torbay and the Start. I and my three brother scouts attached to the station attributed this to spies the other side of Dartmouth, but I think our almost exclusive diet of turnips (fried, boiled, *au naturel* and scrambled) may have reduced our powers of concentration.

Coombe after coombe comes down to the sea, most of them culminating in tiny curving beaches. One of the loveliest of these is at Coleton Fishacre - the estate of the D'Oyly Cartes. Here in this secluded corner they enjoy beauty given across the footlights to crowded operatic audiences.

For a little while I am becalmed in one of the bays. Nothing is in sight but wild cliffs and wilder vegetation. Then, mixing with the cries of the disturbed sea-birds, comes the lowing of cows; what a pleasant homely sound to break in upon this seemingly long separation from the haunts of men! And now, peeping over the storm-twisted thorn bushes of the sea's edge, I glimpse the tops of apple orchards. So just behind that cruel desolate cliff face there is a Devon farmer, probably at this moment gathering his laughing children to their midday meal in the big comfortable kitchen.

Throughout Devon scenery you will find the rich, cultivated homely things side by side with outcrops of something rugged, untamable, starkly elemental; and that quality has become reflected in the characters of Devon Men.

With these reflections in my head it is not surprising that as I approached the once corsair-infested entrance to the Dart I began to scan suspiciously each rocky bay. Suddenly a long black boat with a red flag dashed out from behind a rock and the crash of a broadside reverberated among the jagged cliffs. I rubbed my eyes, but it was not a dream, and I prepared to sell my life dearly. Unfortunately for this story I have to record an anti-climax; for the boat turned out to be a big black barge peaceably engaged in blasting limestone, presumably for Brixham breakwater.

Chapter 2

Along the Dart

I had been so long with thoughts of other times that I had lost all idea of present time, and my watch obligingly chose this occasion finally to succumb to the effects of sea water.

By the pervasive warmth I judged it must be almost afternoon and I began to have fears of missing the tide at the entrance to the Dart. But headland after headland had been passed, and hours, seemingly, had worn on, without my sighting any human habitation. I weathered the next headland. No ship, no habitation, no apparatus of a port, no indication of a river entrance broke the coast. I gazed once more into a secluded bay, virgin, unspoilt, speckled with pines, dark and shadowy in the noonday heat.

Lo, as I was preparing to set a course across to the next headland, there peeped at me from the inmost corner of the bay the friendly sunlit face of Dartmouth Castle! I hailed it with delight and came up to the wind towards it. But I was not at Dartmouth yet! The wind, which had been a strong though fitful helper, rushing down the coombes upon my starboard beam, was caught by the deep valley of the Dart and twisted to blow full in my face. I felt as helpless as a fly trying to enter a sounding trumpet.

Furiously it came, forcing *Sandpiper* again and again onto her beam ends, but inch by inch we fought our way forward, hiding from the worst blasts under the cliffs of Kingswear. At this rate Dartmouth, let alone Dartington, would never see me until nightfall. What had happened to the current? Wind or no wind I must go out and seek it in midstream. With trembling hull and quivering sail *Sandpiper* beat her way into midstream and there, surely enough, I felt the firm grip of the tide and exulted in the power that swung us magnificently into the Dart and would doubtless carry us right up into the hills. Vagabond sailor that I was, I should yet turn up in time to change into a boiled shirt that evening.

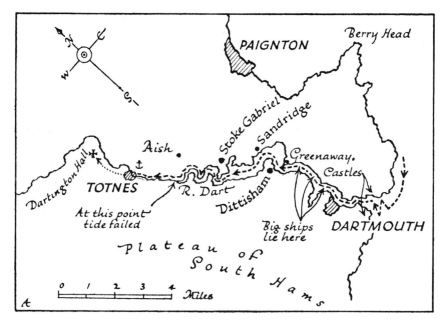

At the moment I thought nothing of such frippery, but only of the incomparable view before me. Poised between the ocean and this silver streak of water winding between cliffs and wooded hills, I knew then that I stood before the loveliest and most navigable gateway to Dartmoor, and I swore to myself to follow it over no matter what obstacles until I should reach the granite and the heather.

Words can only hope to catalogue points of attraction in this vision of the Dart from the sea. Whilst one's senses are bewitched by the bold beauty of sweeping hills one's mind turns to the fierce glamour of its history and the poetry of a charming human habitation lovingly tended through the centuries.

In the deepest cleft of the woods and gorse-strewn cliffs the first human handiwork peeps out - the sentinel castles of Dartmouth and Kingswear on either side of the entrance. Fierce and threatening they doubtless were in their fiery youth centuries ago, and some martial bearing they still have, despite their toy-like beauty, but now they have tuned down to a sweet and comely domesticity, like two pleasant old folk in a Devonshire cottage. Above them tower high ranges of

hills, immense and wooded, within the circle of whose ramparts one glimpses soon the snugly clustering houses of ancient Dartmouth, wrapped in the faint blue haze of chimney smoke. An Italian, sent by Spain to report on Dartmouth as a suitable point of invasion, and asked if its walls were so impregnable, replied "It has no

17

walls; the mountains are its walls".

Swan-like yachts and tall liners lie moored in the deep green pool of the river, and over the town the Royal Naval College, nursery of our Navy, turns a bright and eager face towards the sea.

No wonder that this has been a coveted habitation since history began. No wonder that the Bretons and Dartmouth's other jealous enemies down the centuries found it a place impossible to subdue. At one time the men of Dartmouth and the Bretons tried to make a living by robbing each other. Their favourite recreation became to make a bonfire of each other's houses. Failing in many direct assaults the French thought to land at the quiet little cove of Blackpool and descend on Dartmouth over the hills. The ruse failed because the English, with the espionage service for which they are justly famed, were expecting the raid and were lined up, men and women alike, behind trenches and all manner of diabolical traps, on Blackpool sands. The battle-hungry French knights were soon glad to escape back to their ships. Yet the last laugh was with the Bretons, for under Du Chatel, who was determined to smoke out the "brook of vipers", the town was taken by direct assault a year later and the smoke of its burning poured out of the hollow cauldron of the hills.

A repetition was prevented for all time by the building in 1481, by Edward IV, of the twin castles which still sentinel the river mouth. Henry the Eighth further licensed Dartmouth's piracy, by strengthening these defences with cannon and by insisting that a "strong and mighty chain" be stretched across the river every night after dusk. Thus encouraged in their natural sport the Dartmouthians did yeoman service for their country. The past of Dartmouth is no Sunday School tale, but it is full of the high lights and deep shadows of human life, and rich with colour from the very dawn of history. Did not Chaucer's stout sea captain come from 'Dertemouth'? Calais was besieged mainly by ships out of Dartmouth, then the largest port of the kingdom. William Rufus embarked his army here; and Coeur de Lion, with all his crusaders, said good-bye to England at Dartmouth, seeing in its loveliness the last of the motherland.

On that stormy day when the Armada passed up the Channel, the battered and blood-stained *Madre de Dios* was brought to anchor before the town, a grim but magnificent trophy to assure the anxious mothers and wives that their menfolk out there in the Channel were indeed acquitting themselves like men.

Throughout the Civil War, Dartmouth held out for the King (had it not often been the darling of Kings?), defying attack from land and sea. But in 1646, on one of these January nights that in Devon are so mild they might pass for summer eves elsewhere, the Parliamentary troops, sternly rejecting the seductions of the Devon climate, took the town by surprise an hour before midnight. Only Kingswear Castle held out, and it is said that the two castles continued for weeks to fire cannon-balls at each other across the river, to the great embarrassment of shipping. I can find no historical record of this, but it was described to me by a very old inhabitant so vividly that I scarcely dare to question that he saw it with his own eyes - and I myself have seen many of the rusty cannon-balls that to this day are constantly dug up from the castle garden.

Lest you should think that Dartmouth men have played no part in the constructive and creative life of civilisation I would remind you of her artists and explorers and particularly of the little ironmonger, Newcomen, pondering on power in the quiet valley until he constructed what many consider to be the first real steam engine.

But the present is no time for dreaming or even for drinking in the scenery. *Sandpiper* is scudding across the little waves that are like scrolls of liquid sunshine. She dips and glides like a sea-gull and we have some exciting and even apprehensive moments, for the estuary is deep and the tides are strong. I think of other keels that have ploughed these waters in far worse weather and I look at the near and friendly shore; at the little beaches with children bathing unconcernedly and the splashes of colour where women are languidly sunbathing.

Gaining confidence from the sight of so many fellow-beings at hand once more, I made a hazardous tack right across the river. Arriving by Dartmouth Castle my eye is caught by a blonde damsel in a green bathing costume, lying on a rock reading a book. In spite of the fact that I know all about the Lorelei and can, if not prevented in time, sing about the sad fate of the sailor, I watch the damsel a little too long so that an unseen catspaw of wind throws us on our beam ends. The damsel drops her book and begins to take a keen interest. Alas, that an exhibition of inept sailing should excite a damsel's admiration! Glancing at this Lorelei rock I begin to have serious doubts as to whether it is worth while to sail on to Totnes, which, as everyone knows, is a very ordinary sort of place. The damsel bestows on me a full-blown smile, a smile for which any man would willingly have been wrecked, scuppered, capsized or otherwise cast ashore. Alas, I never received it. At that moment a smart sailing dinghy shot between me and the shore. I never knew where it came from, but it sped along on the opposite tack, skippered by a young naval cadet, who intercepted and carried off the smile which was undoubtedly my perquisite. Indignantly I put ashore and started in pursuit. This embryo admiral gave one contemptuous glance at *Sandpiper* (as is the habit with naval men

looking at longshore boats) as if it were some un-
savoury flotsam brought in by the tide. He hitched his
boat a point nearer to the wind and prepared to leave
me behind. I hung on. We raced in and out of the shipping, and I must say I was surprised to find how *Sandpiper* held her own.

Where the river opens out into the pool by Kingswear
I actually gained on him through keeping to the middle
stream. It is a sound general rule to keep to the
middle of the stream when you want the tide as a helper
and to stick close to the shores, tacking into little
bays, when the tide is against you. The admiral lost a
quarter of a mile through ignoring this, but soon his
faster boat brought him level again. This time as he
passed he gazed upon *Sandpiper* with genuine curiosity.
However, this feature custodian of sea power soon remembered himself and, turning a disdainful back, proceeded to leave us behind.

The centre of the river here has long possessed a
fence of anchored liners and cargo boats - sad reflection on the state of world trade. When my rival passed
to one side of the fence I passed to the other. Dropping my sail under cover of those lofty hulls I proceeded to paddle furiously. Half a mile further I

emerged through a gap in the fence to greet my rival's astonished gaze with a leisurely air of disdain. He never caught me up again, but presently swung to an anchorage and I relaxed from my unphilosophical competitiveness to find that I was almost at Dittisham and had missed much lovely scenery.

Just before Dittisham, sleepy village of damson, plum and apple orchards straggling up the hillside like Rhenish vineyards, the river narrows suddenly and the stream tumbles over a rock in the middle marked by a danger post. At this critical point it was my misfortune to meet an overloaded Dart paddle steamer which I consequently regarded with even more disfavour than usual. If community singing can heighten the appreciation of melody I suppose community viewing can increase the sense of beauty; but my observation suggests that crowds on boats usually divert themselves with parlour games - innocent and otherwise - and look up at the scenery only when the boat comes to the wharf again.

Despite their wash, which nearly upset me, I would not have changed places. One can only feel sorry for those who have to see beauty in such rapid snatches. But through such aids the appreciation of the Dart's loveliness is now widespread. "Eighty years ago", says S. P. B. Mais, "two boatmen tried without success to make a living by rowing visitors up the Dart. In an average August now each of the paddle steamers can count on 20,000 passengers during the month."

Queen Victoria was one of the first outside Devonshire to recognise that this is England's loveliest river, and it was she who gave to it the name of the "English Rhine" - a title which has stuck in virtue of its aptness - though the dimensions of the Dart are dwarfed by the Rhine. It is a comely little maid where the Rhine is a full-breasted Kriemhilda. Fortunately, artists do not measure beauty by a yardstick.

The Dart in my opinion genuinely holds claim to be Britain's loveliest river. It has the quiet garden stretches of the Thames but breaks out towards the sea into a rugged beauty which the Thames cannot claim. It prattles and swirls by lonely moorland heights in a way denied to the Wye. Like the Dee its torrents burst through woods and lonely heather brakes, but its later course has a mellow richness, a noble gentleness, to which the Dee never matures. In this piquant variety and boundless generosity of beauty it is rivalled only by the Erme, a smaller river but a gem beyond prize. Yet the Erme lacks the final touch of man's embellishments.

If artists do not measure beauty by the yardstick, it is even truer that a country's greatness is measured not so much by the number and richness of its lands as by the quality of its men. Lovely Greenaway, on our right, produced a noble harvest in the family of the Gilberts, descendants of that Gislebert who came over with William the Conqueror. Humphrey Gilbert who was born in Greenaway House, hard by the ferry bell yonder, was a half brother of Sir Walter Raleigh. A very high proportion of Devon's eminent men were relatives sprung from the strains of one or two highly gifted families.

After rounding two sharp bends of the Dart we shall come in view of Stoke Gabriel village and before that of Sandridge Park where lived John Davis, lifelong friend of Humphrey Gilbert. In 1585, armed with Gilbert's calculations, he set out in the *Moonshine* of Dartmouth, likewise to seek a north-west passage and to find a market in India and China for West Country woollen goods. With him went the *Sunshine* of London, the *Mermaid* and the *North Star*. The tracks of his voyage may be seen in the great spaces of Northern Canada named after his friends and the places he loved – Gilbert Sound, Exeter Sound, Totnes Road, Mount Raleigh and others. Those names mark the trail of a failure more glorious than many successes. The north-west passage remained a great and daring conception, not to be realised perhaps until the days of air travel.

But stout John Davis returned to the quiet corner of Devon again full of strange tales of the icy breath of the Arctic, of the Northern Lights and especially of a herd of unicorns (probably elks) which he had seen at Cape Desolation. Doubtless on many a summer day such as

this he walked through these lovely woods to pay a call
on Sir Humphrey at Greenaway, to discuss and ponder the
stirring tales about this brave new world which
weather-beaten ships brought in to Dartmouth. Then
Spring comes again and his ships sail out of the Dart
to find their way, successfully this time, by a new
route, to China, to India and round the world, across
the wide Pacific. Alas, the gentle woods, dipping their
branches into the quiet Dart by Sandridge, listened for
John Davis' return in vain. He lies in the wide Pacific
murdered by some misguided Japanese pirates whom he had
saved from shipwreck.

At this point I am faced by my own explorer's problem
being unable to see which is the main stream of the
river, for just below Sandridge it opens into so broad
a stretch of water that its source might be in any
direction. One keeps to the west, avoiding Galmpton
creek, which bites in deeply to the north and even to
the east until it almost reaches the back of Paignton
which we left long ago. Galmpton is a ship-making and
ship-breaking village. Great lifeless hulls stretch
their blackened timbers to the sky as if asking to be
lifted from the slow oozing tide, back to the heaving,
gliding life of the sea.

Now Stoke Gabriel, headquarters of Dart salmon-
fishing, peeps from its tiny creek on my starboard
beam. I have never understood the object of the curious
causeway built across this shady creek and which holds
back so much tidal water. Perhaps it is a fishing
device. The sound of the pouring water after high tide
is a musical background to the quiet life of Stoke
Gabriel. This small village, quaint tangle of cottages
and lanes, is as easy to get lost in as London itself.
I once put up at a cottage there, arriving about seven
in the evening, and, setting out on a ten minutes'
stroll afterwards, I took the rest of the evening to
find my way back to it! Dittisham, across the water
lower down, is little better. There a man climbs up the
hill from the river to the church only to find the
river facing him again!

In the two-mile stretch of fairly straight water

known as "the long stream", the wind held well. I am opposite Bow Creek in little more than an hour after passing Dartmouth, Bow Creek leading to the villages of Ashprington - gem-like Ashprington - Tuckenhay and Cornworthy, villages well worth exploring. Cornworthy is at the end of all creation, for to reach it and the other creek villages you much climb up and down lanes so steep as to appal the most spirited car, and so deep and winding that if it should meet another both will rest there for all eternity. Its squire, who was once a much appreciated schoolmate of mine, used rightly to boast that the view from his fields was worth £1,000 a year. Alas, he cannot afford the luxury of that view now, and Cornworthy is for me a sad village.

The great hills that lift their shoulders on this bank of the Dart are the outer wall of the high table-land of the South Hams which stretches westward across South Devon through Halwell, Kingsbridge and Salcombe to the confines of Plymouth. Casual visitors have been heard to describe the South Hams as the plainest part of Devonshire, but whoever knows Devon well is more likely to call this its very heart; for in its high windswept fields there is a spell which when it claims one, claims for ever. One has the feeling of living on a great dome, rim of a skiey horizon. This generous upheaval of the land is sculptured by deep valleys into forms that never cease to enchant the eye; and the patterned fields with their ever-varying greens and reds and yellows, beguile one as much as the colours of the moor. Equally characteristic are the deep lanes that plunge erratically from the bold, bare hills into the wooded, luxurious and mysterious valleys, always with singing streams. It is a rule that every village is reached by a steep descent and left by an equally steep climb. Most of these villages are little homely affairs of half a dozen thatched cottages.

Although the Dart is only on the eastern edge of the plateau I often think that it embodies the most typical of the South Hams country. Where else is such quiet to be enjoyed? Just now the wind blows faintly and the tide, having almost filled the river to the brim, rests from its labours in a hushed sleep. Far above, the sun illumines the great arches of the hills, but here one peeps into deep valleys of green gloom. Darkling creeks stray off into the mossy woods, surely creeping to the ultimate sources from which all silence and slumber well up into the air.

Occasionally one sights a large farmstead, covered with moss, ivy and lichens, and carved in that serene grey-green stone which abounds there. Towards Totnes or farther west it becomes again the smouldering, ruddy Devon sandstone which makes a rich yet sombre background for all the fresh and verdant hues of foliage.

Every green thing luxuriates here, for the valleys are suntraps, where no storms come and where the gentle voice of running water is the companion of silence. In long, dry summers the streams are still bubbling here, and in the South Hams valleys you will find on the dustiest day little groups of cottages, sleeping in the heat, listening to the lullaby of brooks, with the thatch pulled down over their eyes the better to dream. If the outer worlds get too intrusive or the glare of the sun too harsh they will wrap themselves in soft, silvery, misty rain, which falls like a curtain across the end of the valley, locking out everything which would break in too soon upon oneself and one's thoughts.

As it happens, even the Paignton side of the Dart at this point is almost as undisturbed. Past the mill and up the valley on our starboard beam is the village of Aish in whose tree-shaded lane you will find a cottage called Parliament House, which we have already mentioned as being the place where William III, soon after his landing at Brixham, secretly held his first "Parliament" with those of the local nobility who decided to stand by him. A secret place it is, ideal for a meeting that was practically a conspiracy. High above it is the little ring of trees known as Windmill Beacon and which is quite the most ubiquitous landmark in these parts. Many know the outline of Windmill Beacon but nobody seems to visit Aish, though in its forgotten hollow the destinies of England were once decided.

I am scanning the valley ahead constantly now, hoping
to see Totnes. It is tea-time but there is no tea
aboard *Sandpiper*, and my inner restlessness is matched
by a restlessness in the tide, now all too obviously
beginning to move ever so slightly seaward again. My
communings with the scenery must come to an end: I must
down sail and paddle hard.

In a moment, coming into a straight stretch of river
beyond lovely Sharpham Woods, I recognise the ruins of
Windwhistle Cottage, perched on the hills to starboard
and then, straight ahead, the old red sandstone tower
of Totnes Church itself. Below it cluster the houses of
the steep high street and at the water's edge the cider
and timber warehouses, on the quays which had received
merchandise since the time of Troy.

For Totnes is genuinely but quite unconsciously old.
It was the governing centre of South Devon before
Torquay was a name. It was a flourishing city, with the
privilege of minting its own money before the time of
the Conquest. From its gates the Romans built the Fosse
Way, straight as an arrow through the Midlands and on
to Caithness.

For ought I know *Sandpiper* is sailing where the
Argonauts came in search of the Golden Fleece. At any
rate the inhabitants talk familiarly of the Phoenicians
and will also shew you a stone in the high street
called the Brutus Stone. Historians, however, will not
agree that Brutus stepped ashore there. They call it
the Bruiter's (town crier's) stone instead.

Among the possessions of Totnes one must mention a
lovely view from its river bridge; a quaint old high
street, too steep and narrow for the convenience of
modern cars, a butterwalk; a curious round castle so
cleverly designed with a spiral approach that no one
has ever taken it since it was built at the Conquest; a
house built across the street; and an obelisk to remind
you that the son of a Totnes doctor, Wills, was the
first man to cross Australia.

Memories in Totnes go back easily through the centuries, as is shewn even by the idioms of speech. Lady
Northcote reminds us that the Totnes expression, "Going

to Paignton to meet the French," meaning to meet
trouble halfway, dates from the threatened French invasion of Torbay in 1779. Totnes, nevertheless, does
not advertise its antiquity: it just gets on with the
daily task, content to be a lovable and self-respecting
little town. But, if Londoners wax scornful of its
comparative poverty, it may pertly remind them that its
Mayor, by an ancient custom, takes precedence of the
Lord Mayor of London at all state ceremonies.

By Totnes bridge the stream had set so strongly
against me that I was glad to call the game a draw and
walk the remaining two miles to Dartington. There I
arrived, an hour late, dishevelled and salt-encrusted,
among the spick and span guests. But the thirst which I
had saved up that day was the envy of all beholders.

Chapter 3

The Gateway to Dartmoor

We were equipping an expedition to reach Dartmoor via the Dart, and, remembering the crescendo of obstacles that had eventually brought us to a standstill on the Exe, I knew that the first essential equipment was a companion of iron muscles and indomitable temper. Fortunately the notion appealed greatly to Donald Swan of Dartington, who was as sinewy and as much at home on water as his name might suggest.

The first rapid, under the railway bridge, is an opponent to be reckoned with (note that it doesn't exist at high tide), but Dartington Weir was easily crossed near the right bank (left facing upstream). We had paddled from Totnes veiled in a fine, billowy lace of autumn mist, but above the weir the sun shone brightly on the grounds of Dartington Hall, making such a fine picture that it seemed a pity to leave it for the bleak moors. How variously the trees age into autumn! The elms turn to the yellow of brass; oaks ripen to a dappled gold whilst the ash and willow hang their blond tresses to catch pale reflections in the water. But the scattered hazel bushes were like watch fires and the tall beeches had such ruddy tops that their leaves glowed positively like red rose blossoms against the hard blue of the sky.

But we thought only of the keen air about the granite tors: we imagined *Sandpiper* migrating among the heather of the boundless moors and we pressed on with a vigorous rhythm of our paddles.

Yet, though we pressed straight on, I should like in imagination to turn aside to see what is to be found up that little navigable tributary which winds away from just below the weir through a sea of rushes and enters that steep valley which leads to the unusual old villages of Littlehempston and Broadhempston.

If one follows the valley afoot where it turns back on itself towards the east, one comes to an insignificant village called Berry Pomeroy. Looking at Berry Pomeroy and the lovely castle lost in the woods, you will find it strange to think that (in rivalry with Totnes) this was once the sea of government throughout much of South Devon and, indeed, of the South-West.

On opposite sides of the Dart there have lived since ancient times two noble houses. On the left bank, Berry Pomeroy, possessed by a fierce brood, reactionary in temper, having no aim but its own aggrandisement. On the right bank, Dartington Hall, home of many questing sons who have lived a little in advance of their time and fought to improve the human lot. Berry Pomeroy is a ruin and some memories: Dartington is entering on a new life of experiment and conquest.

What Dartington has become now would be difficult to describe in a few sentences. S. P. B. Mais describes it as an "agriculture college", but that I think was because he saw some cows going about with a harassed expression. It is only to be defined as a social experiment. It is the child of an English schoolmaster and an American millionairess. An attempt to build a rural community on the sound basis of planned and scientific agriculture and crowned with a community life in which art and music and scientific research vie with each other as the cardinal interests. In the beautiful old Elizabethan banquetting terraced lawns you may see men striding deep in thought, who upon acquaintance will be found to be dramatists, scientists, or famous artists, in the throes of creation.

The school, the modern buildings of which stand out valiantly and unashamed from hill and copse, has become

the public school of the intelligentsia. The staff
enforces few or no rules: the children establish their
own discipline, and you may see a young Huxley, a
Freud, a Russell or the children of some famous novelist sitting at class in bathing costume or some other
rig which he happens to consider the best wear on that
day. To-day, one is smoking a clay pipe which he happens to consider at the moment the experiment *par
excellence.*

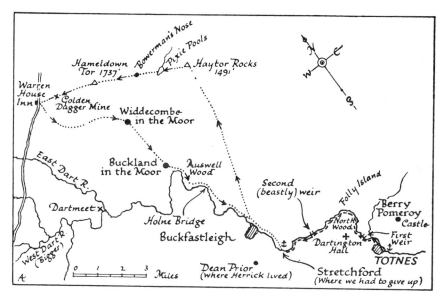

Before the river bends left we run into the first
rapid, by Folly Island, that long drift of sand and
pebbles overgrown by tall fir trees and carpeted in
spring with the richest bluebells. But we do not have
to fight with the rapids long, for in the bathing pool
ahead, half Dartington is enjoying a morning splash
and sun-bathe without any embarrassment by clinging
costumes. At first we are a little uncertain as to who
is who, for it is strangely difficult to recognise your
friends under a nudist regime - the landmarks are so
different.

Yonder, bearded and stalwart figure on the bank is
undoubtedly Vic, though it might well be John the

Baptist. Around him clusters a small circle of naked youths and girls, clean-limbed and lithe, gathering instruction in life-saving. Farther along is apparently Virginia wearing a slip of a bathing costume, either because she is still affected by childhood inhibitions or because she wishes the distinction of being "plus a little something some others haven't got". However she is not ostracised for this weakness or peculiarity as she might be in some nudist communities.

At the sight of our difficulties in the rapids the bathers in the pool rush with yells of welcome to haul us up into smooth water. Acadamy pictures of Ulysses and the Sirens were nothing to this. The prow was seized by two blonde maidens whose gently tanned skin almost matched the golden lights of their hair; three muscular Leanders urged us foaming through the glistening stream; so swiftly that when we came to deeper water little four-year-old Bill had to be gathered aboard to save him from drowning. Thus to his glee he was ferried across the pool sitting on the prow of *Sandpiper* to be duly landed with less venturesome water babies splashing in the shallows by the salmon pier.

Now we raise our paddles in thanks and farewell and leave the bright sunlight to plunge under the shadow of North Wood. And as we go I ask myself, somewhat sadly, why all the estates and beauty spots of this lovely Devon cannot grow into homes of happiness, beauty and culture such as this; communities where one may work and play in an atmosphere of sanity and enterprise. Needless to say, Dartington, to begin with, was more or less wilfully misunderstood by all the neighbourhood. More legends gathered around it in the last ten years than in the previous thousand of its existence. Most deal with the freedom of speech of the children and are quite mythical. One was told to me by a bishop so I suppose it must be true. He knocked on the door which was opened by a pretty little girl of four who had apparently been interrupted in a game. "What the H--- do you want?" she demanded, not repressing her annoyance, lest she should become a catty woman when she grew up. "My God!" exclaimed the bishop with more astonishment than piety. The little girl eyed him with scorn. "You ought to be old enough to know there's no such thing," she exclaimed, and shut the door upon him, which gave him time to think.

Totnes' chief concern was a horror of nudity; a horror so marked that Totnesians on the little train that follows the river to Ashburton nearly tip the train over in their rush to the windows of one side. Thus do enterprises of great pith and moment become known only for their inessentials.

By North Wood the river is extremely beautiful. Even the electricity pylons which stride across the Dart here are transformed into things of delicate beauty, their tracery of design contrasting keenly with the dark, untamed billowing of the wood.

Towards Staverton Bridge, where much of the tasteful Dartington furniture is made, we were held up by frequent rapids, evidently heralding a weir. This weir we

met just before the bridge, a wicked affair with sides
as angular and jagged as the sides of pyramids, and not
set squarely across the river but running almost
lengthwise, taking islands in its stride. On one of

these islands we stopped and ate like wolves. Then we
pressed on, but only to the island above Staverton
Bridge for *Sandpiper* had sprung a leak and had to be
patched. We sat in the long untrodden grass of the
island, waiting for the patch to dry, but we never got
beyond that island, for we unwisely drank all the
bottles of Dartington cider - "to lighten ship," as
Donald explained. The laughter of the water on the
smooth pebbles was infinitely delightful; the afternoon
was warm; the long grass was both a downy pillow and a
Venetian blind to shut out the world. So I found myself
in *Sandpiper,* which had mysteriously grown a pair of
wings and which flew low over the rapids dipping into
pools on its flight. We perched on Haytor which had
apparently become a nesting ground for angels with the
faces of film stars, but every time I tried to reach
them *Sandpiper* pushed me away, so we flew to Cranmere
Pool which was stacked high with cider bottles. Whilst

I was opening the first dozen of these I awoke, to find that it was sundown.

When we left the island next morning there was a keen edge on the air, though the sun flooded the valley and the sky was serenely blue. Braced in this fashion we fought many rocky rapids and a small but obstinate weir, passing through secluded stretches which already had the boulder-strewn character of the moorland river. By the evening we were rewarded by our first glimpse of the moors - it might have been Ryder's Hill - a lofty purple and brown ridge, clear and serene under the wandering cloud shadows. Though it was still far away we welcomed it with the fanatical joy of a pilgrim caravan in sight of Mecca. But when we got out the map we had to face the bitter fact that we had made only two miles of the eight that needed to be covered.

"The water is so low; we must wait until after rain," said Donald with apparently sound reasoning. We debated the matter; whether it is better to have little water and many shallows or few shallows and a roaring catar-act at the rapids. We thought the latter, then, but later we were wetter and wiser. If you have a stout crew get as much water as you can going downstream; but pray for moderate droughts when you scale the river.

In any case it is fatal to ask for rain in Devon-shire. It rained the next day and so on for October and November. During this time it was mild and December was no month for overcoats, but when we were finally able to get to *Sandpiper* again, on Christmas morning, the weather was hard and very frosty.

Even when it is mild and sunny ten miles away at the coast it is frozen and snowbound on Dartmoor. Thus in this county you may enjoy all climates by walking up or down a few hundreds of feet. We had approached the moors near enough to feel their icy breath, and the water which came plunging down the valley was as if from the North Pole.

There is no keeping dry when forcing rapids, though you may improve matters by adopting wading boots and tying your mackintosh tightly at the wrists to stop water trickling past your armpits. But for all these

discomforts   there is a fine zest in winning   your   way
yard by yard against the torrent, climbing higher and
ever higher.

"Onward,   to the moors!" the words echoed in our ears
from the drumming waterfalls and came with our hissing
breath as we paddled desperately against diverting
currents. Verily we should have a finer appetite for
our Christmas dinner than anyone else in Devon! But by
midday we were hiding from each other that confidence
was failing: in two hours we had gained only half a
mile; the rapids were almost continuous, and, to crown
all, *Sandpiper* was leaking again.

We floundered over slippery boulders; tugging and
heaving, whilst the overhanging trees shut out the
waning light of the short day and dripped ceaselessly
upon our sweating brows. A damp, icy mist oozed out of
the woods. "Onward," we groaned, and tore fresh rents
in *Sandpiper's* sorely tried hull. Our clothing stuck to
us with sweat and icy water. In the stiller pools an
edge of ice cut at our hands, whilst flakes of ice were
constantly washed down upon us in the stream.

I thought then, with a glimmer of understanding, of
those men in distant parts of the Empire, who battled
up unknown headwaters in the interests of exploration
and conquest. General Gordon, who smiled at most obstacles, speaks strongly of the great rapids of the
Nile. "I am really quite exhausted", he confesses,
"more mentally than physically. It has been a fearful
day . . . it is the violent eddies that are so ter-
rible."

What Donald wrote in that inevitable diary of his I
don't know; but that day was written in my muscles and
sinews for months and in my bones perhaps for years.
"To the moors!" my heart still sang, but brain and
muscle answered "No!" It was at Stretchford that we
met the obstacle which finally brought us to a standstill.

A fast, deep rapid, dropping a couple of feet and
staked by a great rock in the middle! A slow deep rapid
one can paddle against and a swift shallow one can be
waded. We were nearly 'all in', but we gathered up our

forces and rushed it. True and straight *Sandpiper* flew for the centre of the rapid and the waters struck down on her, filling her almost to sinking, so that we drifted back in the spirit of a decimated cavalry charge. We were done: we should never sail to the moors!

On the bank we cursed the damp and the cold and the boulders and this traitorous Devonshire which had given way to Arctic conditions just when we needed her gentlest winter manners.

Looking at the dripping woods and the rapid flinging its frosty water untiringly into our faces, it was hard to believe that in a few months all would smile again in leaf and flower and sparkling, sunlit water. We would wait for the spring and then continue our journey by boat or foot to our predestined goal.

And as the next day broke sunny and clear, though bitterly cold, we decided to tramp over a part of the moors not included in our main expedition, namely, the eastern moors by Haytor and Widecombe.

First we made for Buckfastleigh but not actually to go into it, for this shameful townlet has stepped out of the ranks of Devon villages by selling its soul to machinery and manufacturing serges and blankets, ay, and munitions of war. It has a Lamb Pie Fair at Midsummer and a Pear Pie in September, but coming from a place like Buckfastleigh these would give any true Devonian a pain in the stomach. It rejoices also in an Abbey which tries to look old but is obviously as new as Woolworths. When Henry "disillusioned the monasteries" a foundation was left here, and in 1882 some French Benedictine monks bought the site, on which they have recently completed a building.

The waters of the Dart must curl into cynical little smiles at having to flow past three such very different institutions in so short a distance - first Buckfast Abbey with its attempt to revivify a past age; then Dartington with its free and intelligent children trained for a constructive life of peace, and finally Dartmouth Naval College whose sons are hardened to be dogs of war to protect alike the ancient and modern, the intelligent and the cloistered.

We reached Haytor to find it wrapped in snow, and in the quarry pools below it a young moorman was enjoying a solitary skating party (though that day some not very hardy people - sane people like you and me - were bathing at Torquay). From this quarry came the granite for London Bridge and for those pillars in the crowded British Museum Reading Room at which one may gaze and float away to lone and desolate moors.

From the rock itself we headed north-westwards to the head of Becka Brook with its lovely waterfalls and Pixie Pools so fine for bathing in summer. ("Becky Falls" to which the motor coaches go is further down, where the brook meets the main road.) We climbed the ramparts of Hound Tor; that most picturesque of Tors which has figured in two British films: "The Hound of the Baskervilles" and that drama of rare loveliness and power, "A Cottage on Dartmoor".

At the queer idol of Bowerman's nose we start to cross the great sombre ridge of Hameldown Tor. At the top we are seventeen hundred feet up and the air is keen. On the northern end we pass large hut circles, some long grass-grown barrows and one still more curi-

ous reminder of the ancient folk who lived their savage
lives up on the moor before the dawn of history. This
was a double row of large slabs, not unlike headstones
of graves, pointing towards the sunrise. Are these
stone rows the successive memorials of a long dynasty
of ancient kings?

Dropping down towards the little ribbon of road we
come to the huge stone circle of Grimspound, the best
preserved and the largest of these fortresses of primitive men. It encloses some practically intact and very
massive hut circles which must have been the 'Bucking-
ham Palace' and 'Bank of England' of that settlement.

Some people let their troubles sink into perspective by considering the sublime distances of the stars; but you may do the same and with a more touching sense of human destiny, by sitting awhile in the silence among these ancient habitations. These stones were hearths and beds before the oldest of cathedrals was thought of; before Rome was built; before the Greeks sailed to Troy; probably before the Pyramids were designed. They belong apparently to the early bronze age; though most of their work was still in chipped and polished stone.

The tribes were, according to all evidence, a very peaceful people, for few weapons are found except on the outer edge of the moor. They looked down on the great expanses of forest-covered and beast-infested lowlands and shunned them. They lived here in enormous numbers so that it is difficult to imagine on what they subsisted. Presumably the winter climate was kinder then than it is to-day. Evidently they thought much of the dead and hauled great granite blocks across the moors for their memorials, which have lasted down the ages as a witness to their spirit.

Over the next ridge, according to our calculations, was Warren House Inn. Faithful to expectations it peeped up over the long hillside, and there we rested on weary limbs. True we had not covered any great distance but a mile on the moors is worth three elsewhere, even when the ground is drier in summer, or frozen hard as now. My friend and guide, Dr. Malim, whose book, *The Romance of Dartmoor,* is the fruit of many years' loving acquaintance with the moor in all its moods, thinks nothing of thirty miles, and has been known to claim forty, in a day.

Hereabouts you will look into steep valleys the sides of which are rudely scarred as by the clawings of a monstrous tiger. These are the "tin streamings". And indeed there was a certain tigerish ferocity about those old tin miners, both in their lawless life out here on the moors and in the relentless way in which they tore the precious metal from the bowels of the earth. I say lawless, but they were a law unto themselves, regulating themselves by their own Stannary

Parliament, recognised by the Crown, and held at certain seasons around the granite seats of Crockern Tor, only a few miles from here.

Down the hillsides run the great tin streamings which time and weather soften but cannot efface, and in the valleys, as in many valleys of Dartmoor, are the ruins of workings belonging to all periods from the time of the Phoenicians to yesterday - or to be precise, to twenty years ago when the discovery of richer deposits in islands eleven thousand miles away from here - Malaya - closed these workings, probably for ever. Now, in the Golden Dagger mine, over which we sit in silent rumination, the great water wheels, and the cottages and the buildings which for a short while at the end of the War housed modern machinery - all are crumbling alike into the soft green surface of the moor. The shafts, down which a boulder will still fall interminable seconds before the last hollow report floats up like a groan from the granite tomb, will also close up in time until they are little bigger than the burrows, like badger holes, into which the slaves were sent with their baskets in the time of Phoenicia and perhaps Ulysses.

At the Warren Inn, beside the peat fire which has never been out for a hundred years, we drank with a little, sociable, white-haired man - the 'Silvertop' of a certain moorland novelist. He is the guardian of the lonely tin mines and in summer a cheery and informative guide for visitors who wish to essay the difficult journey to Cranmere Pool.

Thence, on the following day we circled south to Widecombe in the Moor, which still holds many such cheery souls as Uncle Tom Cobley and those friends of his in the lilt of 'Widecombe Fair'. Wise and favoured with an indomitable good humour are these men who have made and maintained a village in this lovely but granite-hearted countryside. Their very church has been struck by the mountain lightning more times than I can tell and in 1638 the thing happened during Sunday service when the whole village was present, killing four of the congregation and injuring sixty-two. They must have gained a certain sense of humour even in regard to the Divine Providence.

From Widecombe it is only three or four miles to Buckland in the Moor, loveliest of heather-thatched villages. We skirted Buckland Beacon through the deep, enthralling shadow of Ausewell Wood. To tread quietly there, for the practical reason that much of it is private (though the generous owners will not think it necessary to remind you with any disfiguring notice boards) but also because, from the foaming river at its foot to its crown of granite crags, it has the loveliest, enchanted, fairy-story quality I have ever met. Whether you wander beneath the gaunt branches of winter, or stand amazed before the mist of bluebells in spring, or lose yourself in the exuberant undergrowth of summer, it is a fairy wood. Towards Spitchwick and Holne Bridge, moreover, you will find a gnome's cottage, quaintly built of moss and rounded stone in the deepest shadow of the wood. Strangest of all it bears upon its door the number 10 which, since it obviously cannot be the prosaic number of a house in a street, must be some cabalistic sign the deep significance of which is known only to Dartmoor Pixies.

Chapter 4

Dartmoor the Unknowable

In the very centre of Dartmoor is a pool - at least it is called a pool though those gentle folk who visit it only in summer are apt to complain about the tide being out. Hardy moormen like Dr Malim, however, who reach it in the depth of winter, will tell those summer butter-flies of quite an extensive sheet of ice.

Nevertheless I will not deny that you are likely to be disappointed by its appearance, as one generally is on first seeing celebrated things. For Cranmere Pool is certainly celebrated, not because of any material greatness in the spectacle, but because, like the North Pole, it is difficult of attainment and confers a kind of spiritual decoration - an admission to the noble company of Cranmerians - on those who can claim the intelligence and the endurance necessary to know it.

For those who love Devon it has something of the holiness of a pilgrim's shrine; since from this lonely heart well out most of the fair rivers of Devon, greeting the sea by Dartmouth, Plymouth and Barnstaple; feeding rich lands to the north and the south, to east and west.

Finally there is, for all who have learnt the value of solitude, a recurrent appeal in its utter remoteness from all roads and habitations, a lesson in its scorn-ful obliteration of the works of man, and a rare beauty in the harmonious communion which this seemingly bound-

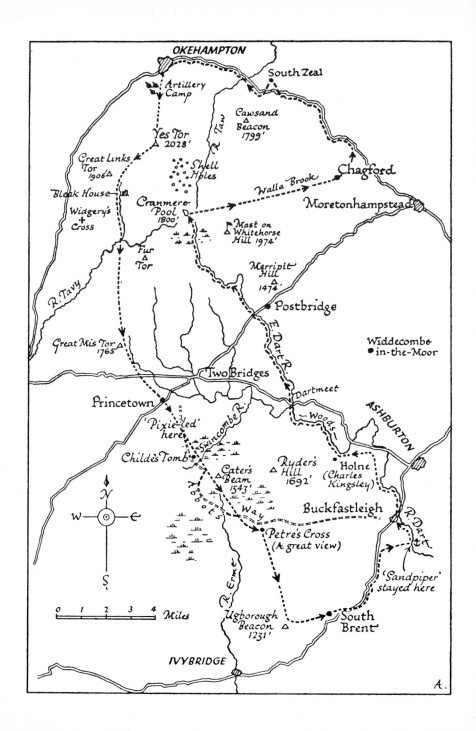

less wilderness holds with its brother the boundless sky.

How shall you essay to reach it? There is a nursery run from Okehampton; a more difficult route up the Walla Brook from Batworthy near Chagford and a somewhat stiffer route from Postbridge or the Warren House Inn; though in the latter case you may enjoy the service of Silvertop as a guide. The veteran's route - difficult, boggy, but offering superb scenery - is from Lydford. People who do things differently have been by aeroplane, though no one has dared to land. And once my brother, with fellow lunatics of the Torbay Motor Club, set out in winter to reach the pool on motor-cycles (they lost them in the snow).

Our route obviously lay up the Dart, which *Sandpiper* had unfortunately refused to scale farther - and this is one of the most difficult but most lovely and varied approaches. It was July and the bogs had dried up as much as they ever do. The sky was cloudless and the air, still bracing in spite of the heat, was rich with the scents of heather and peat. We were four, not counting the dog and the bottles of cider. Dr Reginald, son of Dr Malim the Moor-rover, golden-haired Popsy who nearly lost a fiance when Hugh sailed with me from Exmouth, Jean, shortly to obtain second mate's ticket on *Sandpiper,* and myself.

The expedition set off doing about fifty strides to the minute (except for Pongo the dog who did fifty per sniff). At this rate we were glad to pause for the view at Holne Bridge, which is pretty good in any case, and again for cider in Holne village, which is also pretty good. Charles Kingsley is a son of Holne and the tameless beauty of the place may have done much to produce that rugged soul. The world, alike of the philosopher and the lusty youth, owes much to the man who gave us *Westward Ho!* and *Hereward the Wake.*

Still bent on cutting off the bend of the river we climbed over Holne Reservoir, a warm blue eye in the face of the moor, weeping the softest moorland water to Paignton. Then we began a steep descent through mossy, boulder-strewn woods to the river, foaming gloriously

some hundreds of feet below us. All the way to Dartmeet
one or both banks of the cleave is richly wooded and
beset with the prettiest of streams; but the going is
hard.

So hard that presently we stopped by a pool below a
waterfall and bathed in clear water the colour of wine.
It resembles wine in more than colour: I know of no
bathing which gives such intoxicating freshness as that
beneath the crystal streams of the moors.

We avoided Dartmeet itself because of the brood of
motor coaches which nests there and which might have
necessitated our donning shirts again. To avoid this
we essayed the rough climb up Sharp Tor and so passed
up the East Dart by Yar Tor and Riddon Ridge, arriving
in time to eat mightily at Post Bridge. There we
lounged away a mellow evening on the huge stones of the
Old Clapper Bridge, wondering by what miracle they had
been transported thither before the days of machinery.

On the following day a blazing sun watched the expedition forging ahead again up the East Dart, the
broad valley of which sloped upwards interminably
towards that lofty plateau on the dome of which lies
Cranmere pool, the highest water in Southern England.
A shower-bath under a waterfall gave us renewed energy,

though it cost us a copy of *The Times* which Reginald had brought, thinking that if we got lost for some months we should not be without reading matter. Duly separated, it now made excellent bath-towels for four. The leading article we carefully set aside, but unfortunately Pongo swallowed it, which is more than most people are prepared to do nowadays.

When one emerges on the plateau it is a matter of saying good-bye to the last landmark, in this case the resignation which I reciprocated by falling flat on my back - "beat to the wide". And then Pongo, who had gone ahead by sheer momentum, not to say doggedness, set up a joyous barking, from some invisible hollow. He had found the posting box at Cranmere and with it the scent of human beings, after a desert of purely vegetable odours, which, as every dog knows, are scarcely worth smelling.

Thus we came to Cranmere and signed the massive book. Some visitors are evidently so crazed by their hardships that they burst into verse in this book, but the most frequent cry of all is an appeal for a glass of beer, at any price. A vain cry when six miles of trackless moor separate one from the nearest habitation.

Having no letters with us to post and stamp with the Cranmere stamp we had to fall back on the barbaric custom of stamping our chests - a fine tattoo it made - though Popsy, Jean and Pongo refused to receive their decorations.

If we were to get clear of the moor before nightfall it was necessary for us to leave in half an hour. We lay on the spring heather, drinking in the silence and the sunlight. Only the wind, which never ceases up here on the roof of Devonshire, wailed through the grasses as if striving to tell some sad story which our ears could never quite grasp.

Now we struck off almost due east by Taw Head and Watern Tor, making for Batworthy and Chagford. In the bogs here we passed many bleaching bones, of hapless sheep, bullocks and horses lost in mires or perchance stung by adders. Human bones have been found on the moors ere now, of people caught by sudden fogs wandering in circles till starvation or the bitter cold of the nights slew them.

It is an intriguing experience to be caught by the sudden descent of a moorland mist, through which normally one can see for about thirty yards. But after a time the isolation of one's tiny world begins to become oppressive, for the moor without its views is an extraordinary monotony of dripping boulders, impeding gorse and sudden holes in the ground. For safety, it is necessary only to keep moving downhill, to pick up a stream and follow it to civilisation; but the going may be hard and very wet. In the flattish centre of the moor it is not so easy, for one can scarcely tell which is downhill. That is the dangerous region.

We should have reached Batworthy in full daylight had not Pongo found a rabbit warren only a mile from our goal. Twice we turned back to fetch him and twice he howled out his anguished soul at being torn between loyalty to his friends and what he evidently considered his life purpose. Dusk was falling when we left him, a small white ghost flitting among the rabbit holes, devoted to some higher purpose of the doggy world. But the old Pongo, limping and very muddy, caught us up again at Batworthy, having evidently decided against the life of a hermit in the wilderness.

The roads around the moor are all very erratic, but along none have I been so near to destruction as when driving from Moretonhampstead to Bovey Tracey on a foggy night. G K Chesterton will tell you that "a rolling English drunkard made the rolling English road", and certainly most Devon roads are in the tracks of men drunk with the peculiarly expansive drunkenness of cider. But the moorland roads, bounded by their rambling but massive granite boulder walls, are undoubtedly laid down in the tracks of a very wayward Dartmoor pixie, probably chasing a butterfly. They are full of the maddest caprices, swerving suddenly to avoid a gorse bush, turning back to dip in a cool brook - now side-stepping for no reason on earth and forever shieing at their own shadows. Wherefore, the hour being late, we were of a mind to stay in Chagford or Moretonhampstead rather than drive home.

But Chagford, and still more Moretonhampstead, are not of Devon. Around them the red earth loses its fire, becoming a dead brown colour and nourishing a pale and obedient grass like that which grows in London or Leicestershire, quite unrelated to the shining blue-green flame which sweeps Devon hills. Moretonhampstead is getting some reputation as a sanatorium and admittedly its air is intoxicating, but not so intoxicating as to blind one to Moretonhampstead's deficiencies - a second Newton Abbot, with the same prominence of railway line, and this time without the kind anaesthetic atmosphere of the Teign Valley.

Along the same road we worked our way around the north-eastern edge of the moors next day. Few points of the moor are so justly praised by connoisseurs as that above Belstone, where the Taw Valley rambles up to Steeperton Tor. But we turned off the main road away from Belstone to the old Oxenham Arms at South Zeal. A grand old inn it is, looking as if someone had built it out of an ancient Stonehenge of granite blocks.

Here we won ourselves several glasses of the best through playing darts with three rather awkward yokels.

Taw Marsh

The landlord, however, casually let fall that they were actually County Medical Officers looking for mental defectives, which are said to be numerous in these parts, so we departed quickly to Okehampton.

Thence on the following morning we started on the longest stretch of uninterrupted moorland that is to be found - from Okehampton to Princetown, taking Yes Tor, very nearly the highest point in England south of the Peak district, in our stride.

For ages we climbed, past the Artillery Camp, until we reached the dominating crown of rocks which is Yes Tor and which seems many miles farther from Okehampton than the map indicates. A great gale of wind was blowing from the south-west. The sighing of the wind through the heather and coarse grasses, is a constant companion on the moors, but this was different; it was a howling force which pushed into one's face like an out-thrust hand and cut through one's clothes icily for all its moderate temperature. We did not let it deter us from climbing the mast on Yes Tor and gazing at the incomparable view into the blue distances of the plain of North Devon, Cornwall, the sister heights of Exmoor, Somerset and the Atlantic, on the hazy blue of which I could detect Lundy Island, nearly sixty miles away.

Thence we plunged down into the Okement Valley and so strode on along the great tors - Great Links Tor,

Amicombe Hill, Hare Tor - which stand out so nobly as the western wall of the moor when seen from the plain below. A wild moor this, cut by the deep valleys of the Tavy tributaries, chiselled and abraded by the ceaseless onset of the south-west wind, with its drenching storms of rain, and blustering gales. The granite tors stand out more sharply and more white in colour than elsewhere, whilst the attack on the moors by man, by the tin streamers of Lydford, peat workers and others, seems likewise to have been more violent, for one is seldom free from signs of their penetration and comes upon extensive ruins - as of the workings by Bleak House - in the most remote and desolate valleys. At Grey Tor, there is a cross, erected by Widgery, the elder of those two Widgery's whose paintings of the moors achieve their spirit as no others do. That cross, by its artistic placing, adds a final touch to a most noble piece of scenery.

We crossed the Tavy Gorge after lunch, still going strongly, and rested for a while on Lynch Tor, whence we could see to the westward the slopes of Gibbet Hill, overlooking the Tamar. Though in the unhappy past many

Widgery Cross

an unlucky man may have gazed without enthusiasm on the
view from Gibbet Hill, it is yet as fine an elevation
as any I know within a stone's throw of a main road
from which to see the moors, the valley of the Tamar,
Plymouth, Launceston, the Moors of Bodmin and the adjacent lands of Cornwall. In the immediate foreground
is quaint little Brentor, also rising to a thousand
feet and capped with a tiny church about which many
legends exist.

   Of these the most true-seeming (though that is not
saying much) is the story that the church was built by
a merchant sailor, who, caught in a great storm as he
approached Plymouth, swore to build a church on the
first piece of land he should sight, if God would
deliver him to safety. The first land he sighted was
the high peak of Brentor, far inland. According to my
own limited experience the first land one sights is Lee
Moor and Penn Beacon, but perhaps these were shrouded
in rain or mist when our sailor approached the Eddystone. Or since a church on Lee Moor would find no
congregation perhaps the clergy convinced him that in

the excitement of the moment his bearings were incorrectly taken.

In a while we crossed tracks which Reginald recognised, from his father's description, as being the Old Lich Way (German *Leich* - corpse) - the way along which the moormen had to bring their dead for burial in the churchyards of Mary Tavy or Lydford. The associations of the moor hereabouts are not such as are calculated to brighten the spirits of people wearied by the longest straight trek which it is possible to make, without meeting roads or habitations, across Dartmoor - or indeed anywhere in England. For on passing over the heavy ground of the Great and Little Mis Tors we came in sight of the grey drabness of Princetown Prison, a spectacle which one writer has aptly called "the ugliest thing physically and morally on the moor".

Apart from this grim reminder of the wars with France and with America and with criminal evil in our own population, Princetown is a pleasant little place. Yet in our hatless and mud-bespattered condition we were made uncomfortably aware that Princetown's suspicion and fear of escaping convicts never really sleeps.

From Princetown, Reginald was called back next day to his patients and I might well have made the whole journey to South Brent alone, had I not met at the outset a Dartmoor Pixie, with red hair, a shade more fiery than the tawny bracken, and sharp blue eyes, incalculably mischievous, as lively as the wind-whipped pool beside which I found her. My way lay to the south-east over Fox Tor and through the heart of the southern moors, not a bit of which I should know until I reached Brent Moor. My new-found companion, it appeared, knew the adjacent moor thoroughly and since Excelsior-like, I insisted upon going on, she at length (to my secret relief and admitted delight) agreed to accompany me on the first step, namely to Fox Tor.

There is a bleak unkindness about the great hills around Princetown which is found nowhere else on the moor. The Dartmeet area has just such round-topped tors and precipitous valleys but they are clothed with rich woods and threaded by foaming, pearly streams. Yes Tor and the High Willhays are at an even greater and colder altitude, but in their sweeping curves there is an inherent nobility, a spiritual loveliness which holds one in instant communion. The Cranmere region is quite as monotonous and unbroken in its desolation, yet it is rendered entrancing by some magic which broods there. Perhaps the dour work of man at Princetown has driven the spirits of the moor away: at any rate, I know nowhere else where the moor can be so starkly oppressive and forbidding.

But that morning the air was like champagne. The wind blew gustily, bringing occasional ragged clouds and squalls of rain across the sun-bathed moor and we quickly left the influence of Princetown behind. My pixie had a pretty Celtic wit and I was not altogether surprised when I found she was newly graduated in philosophy. Perhaps she loved these moors because her Celtic ancestors called them home so many centuries ago. At any rate she could not share my coarse Saxon joy in buffeting waves or my love of the rich, wooded creeks of the lowlands. She lived best in the thinner, colder air of high places and appreciated most the mysterious silences of the granite tors or the swift play of cloud shadows on the subtle colours of the moor.

There is a road of excellent surface, as moorland roads go, running for three miles, until one comes in sight of Fox Tor. Here a difference of opinion arose between the Pixie and myself; for I wanted to go direct across Fox Tor Mire and the upper valley of the Swincombe River, which opens like a deep bay into the

hills, inviting a short cut across its surface, whilst my companion said one must go round via Nun's Cross. I, moreover, was curious to visit Childe's Tomb, which lies on the straight route to Fox Tor and the little stone cross of which I could see even at this distance, standing like a lighthouse in the waves which passed over the long, sunlit grass of the heathery valley. Childe who knew the moor well was hunting at Mis Tor when a blizzard overcame him and night descended. To such lengths can the fight go to keep alive our warm specks of life in a great indifferent coldness, that, in the end he killed his horse and crept inside its disembowelled body to gain warmth and protection from the endless, biting snowstorm. But days later he was found dead and was buried there on the moor where he had loved to be.

As we pushed out across the valley we were forced more and more to the north-east by streams and squelchy morasses, until at last we stood hemmed in by water on almost every side. And there a driving rainsquall struck us. The pixie face of my companion expressed a mischievous triumph. We got back with difficulty to firm ground.

"Foolish man," she said, "won't you ever learn to enjoy the moor by sitting in the sun, sheltered from the wind, listening and watching?" But I thought of myself striding through the wind, over the springy turf of the hill-tops, finding all manner of new and wondrous objects in the unknown piece of moor beyond the hills ahead.

"I shall go alone," I replied tersely. "Maybe I shall find my way better alone!"

Her eyes were momentarily ruffled like a moorland pool beneath a squall of rain. She sat cross-legged like an elf on a boulder and her small pointed pixie chin turned indifferently away from me. "Au Revoir," she said simply, smiling at the sun.

When I returned half an hour later very wet and hot and muddy, she still sat there, but lo! she had conjured from the empty moor another male companion, apparently a farmer boy. She left him and joined me in my walk around the rim of hills that half-circled the uncrossable valley.

"You're a very headstrong young man," she laughed. "I expect you get into lots of trouble."

"I wouldn't have missed that view down the valley for anything," I said. "It was worth it."

"Sentimental as well as headstrong," she sighed sadly.

At the ruins of Fox Tor Farm she sat down. "Where will you find a lovelier spot than this", she asked, "in which to spend a summer day?"

I began to feel unaccountably angry. Her face, for all its youth, bore, in my eyes, the wizened inhuman detachment of the true pixie.

"Are you leaving me to find my way back to Princetown alone?" she teased. Oh, wicked, cheating pixie, I thought, but said nothing, for pixies are perhaps not to be judged by human standards. I took a last glance at her intriguing, secretly-smiling eyes, at her impertinent tip-tilted nose and said "Good-bye" very firmly.

As I turned off into the wind and the sun I felt a strangely profound relief at escaping that inscrutable smile, as one escaping from a spell.

But almost at once a drenching rainstorm fell on me as from nowhere and I turned to look back for the pixie to see if she had brought it upon me by incantations, but she had vanished into thin air - the ruins were deserted - neither did I see her again.

It might, of course, have been a natural shower, despite its appalling wetness; for this corner of the moor, near Princetown, gets eighty to ninety inches of rain a year, so badly does it tear the sky with its sharp ramparts. Those who live in London and the eastern counties with twenty-five inches think Torquay damp with thirty-six. Torquay, however, thinks of Okehampton as a really wet spot with nearly double its own rainfall - sixty-one inches. But Princetown is still wetter, with eighty-seven inches, and doubtless the spot on which I stand has to soak up ninety inches of rain in a year.

How infinitely lovely, how superb in its lofty dig-

nity, is this great upland, sweeping in sombre curves,
all at much the same elevation, from Cater's Beam to
Ryder's Hill. Remote as Cranmere from roads, and far
less visited, it stands like an impregnable fortress,
guarded by its ring of far-flung morasses. How near one
is to the sky! Now at my feet, as I crossed Green Hill,
lay the sources of the Avon and the Erme, whilst over
Langcombe Head, yonder, lay the great marsh, two miles
long, from which the Yealm starts its course to the
sea. The most beautiful of these sister rivers is the
Erme. For eight miles it plunges through the loveliest
moor and wooded cleaves, bathed in the sun and rollick-
ing in freedom. Then it meets sober Ivybridge and a
big main road, becomes demure and slips quickly over
the three miles of cultivated country to the next main
road. With that, having done its duty by civilisation
it turns fay again at Flete Castle and plays through
four miles of wild tidal creeks, wooded and bird-
haunted, before finally marrying the sparkling ocean at
Bigbury Bay. But of that tidal stretch we shall learn
more, approaching with *Sandpiper* from the sea. Lithe
and lovely is the Erme, 'sweet seventeen' among the
eastern rivers of Devon. From this eminence one's eye
could range down the whole length of her sinuous form
almost to the sparkling sea.

Ahead is the smooth white cone of a china-clay dump
with a cluster of buildings around it, but it is an
hour before I reach it for I flounder in an extensive,
a subtly extensive, bog, around the upper stream of the
Avon. An hour's walking in a Dartmoor bog region will
give you not only duck's feet but a duck's neck; for,
with the eyes bent relentlessly to the ground one
forgets that the sky exists and acquires a duck's habit
of looking only into watery depths.

The most comical little single-track railway runs
from the clay works, contour-chasing southwards and I
was to run across its naively open track and miniature
but highly self-important signals and junctions several
times in my southward course to Ugborough Beacon. Apparently, all is disused and falling into decay. In a
few years the moor will eat away the wood and metal and

mercifully cover everything with peat and heather. For, as many moormen have observed, the storms and rains and perhaps the chemical qualities of the peat or the saline air from the sea cause the moors to be rapidly destructive of any neglected building, making the pomp of yesterday look like a ruin centuries old. Undoubtedly the moor has an implacable jealousy for any structure other than its own imperishable monuments.

Now I strike the Abbot's Way which is marked by stone crosses at long intervals, one to guide you as each new horizon appears. This toilsome way led from the Abbey at Buckfast to that at Tavistock and was taken in days when one's money and even one's life were not safe on the highways below - but what a dangerous route, beset with mists and bogs, in the depth of winter!

How quiet it was at Petre's Cross! The wind had died down and the blue sky was looped by a few silky cirrus clouds. Feeling the toughest part of the journey was behind me I sat with my back to the big granite stones and thought on all things under the sun. There is nothing like a day on the moors alone for anyone who has forgotten or become frightened to think. One is left face to face with facts from which, down below there, one may be distracted for years by the toys of this world.

But the view must be enjoyed too and I know of no place on the moors that gives so wide a view, though Haytor and the eastern moors perhaps rival Petre's Cross. To the east one looks down to the valley of the Teign and the Exe. To the west one looks upon Plymouth and Cornwall, whilst to the south, save for the portion obscured by Ugborough Beacon and White Barrows, the whole panorama of South Devon is laid out. To see that last panorama in exquisite detail you have only to walk to Ugborough Beacon, the last bulwark of the moors. Northwards and shining in the sun, is the Sheepstor reservoir of Plymouth and a hint of Tavistock and Launceston. Surely there is no other point in Devon from which you can see east and west so many miles or cover so many towns and cities in a glance! It is indeed a great place for a chair of philosophy.

At White Barrows, in spite of the good auguries of the sky at Petre's Cross, a great pall of black cloud threatened and I descended prematurely from the heights, curving down to Shipley Bridge - sedate little beauty spot on the bubbling Avon. But the storm vanished - and I crossed the Bala brook to climb along the far flung crest of Ugborough Beacon.

Thus, in evening calm, I gazed upon the friendly face of the lowlands again; upon the crazy pavement of warm fields and snug villages, the look of which I had almost forgotten though I had been a moorman for barely a week. Though the moors were black with shadow the lowlands reflected back at me the intense golden light of the sinking sun, a liquid gold which spoke of more wind and rain on the moors to-morrow. Nevertheless, I would have liked to have made that journey again on the morrow: for it is the secret of the charm of Dartmoor that one never gets tired of it. With all the granite permanence of its heart it is yet always changing, responding with fresh life to each fresh direction of approach, so that even to the man who spends his life there it is essentially unknowable.

The darkening moors hurried me on, as if anxious to shut out strangers from the pixies' midnight revels. Doubtless too that night the packs of the Yeth Hounds would run from tor to tor, with blue flame floating from their mouths. Yet these are things that only the oldest moormen may see. I hurried on, a little fearfully. In the last half-hour of light I dropped a thousand feet in little more than a mile and found myself on the South Brent road, a few miles from Dartington, amidst the warm lowlands, with their tidal rivers conveying the tang of the sea.

Chapter 5

Dart to the Start

Spring is a very early visitor in Devon and earliest of all she comes to the river valleys and the deep coombes of Dart, Yealm and Avon, nestling by the southern coast. Often she steps into the dance of the seasons before autumn has dragged her skirts from the stage, thus leaving hoary winter standing in the wings, sadly unemployed for years on end.

But such a spring is not like the fay, maddening maiden with flashing curls of brazen sunshine, who rushes belatedly into northern climates. She has rather a shy, ethereal quality, this gentle spring who slips in before her time, to kiss the faded lips of the dying old year. And later, when the calendar calls for spring, this gentle, dark-eyed creature is already beguiling the land of her choice with the warm and languorous smiles of summer.

In March there was a sparkling shiver of sunlight on the river and *Sandpiper* tugged fitfully at her moorings, tired of the protected wooded recesses, of the smell of mouldering leaves and the sound of lowing cattle. She felt the promised warmth of spring, smelt the brine brought thither by the spring breezes, and longed for the heave and the glide of open water. Somewhere a stretch of coast was calling her as it was calling me - a stretch of coast southward to the Start Lighthouse and the southernmost headlands of Devon.

But out ethereal spring does not lack the love of practical joking possessed by all English weather. On the first of April it rained - warm rain, but about three drops to the pint - and the shower lasted for a week.

When I went down by North Wood the Dart was a foaming flood, seven or eight feet above its normal level, red with the spoil of invaded meadows, bursting towards the sea, bearing logs, young trees, granite sand, and all the debris of moor and woodland.

The wooden post at Dartington, bearing notches to mark the height of other floods, which come between January and April, was itself almost submerged, and *Sandpiper* herself was gone! I rushed towards the weir, breaking through hedges, shaking the young green shoots and the dripping hazel catkins, hoping some overhanging tree had arrested her impatient escape. No sign. And the weir was a proud and toppling arch of thundering foam, awakening awe in one who had known only contempt for summer weirs.

With the subsiding waters, however, *Sandpiper* rewarded my obstinate faith in her reappearance. She thrust an undaunted burgee above the water and I found her filled with mud but otherwise none the worse for her dive to the river bed.

In this disgustingly muddy state she was introduced to Jean, who had just signed on as the mate for the next cruise - a cruise which lasted, I may say, until every inch of Devon coast had been explored and until *Sandpiper,* in spite of Jean's cherishing care, had become too decrepit to sail on anything but the pond of a pleasure ground.

In spite of Jean's athletic build and her invincible good humour our passage down the Dart was not in the best cruising tradition; for Jean started with a lamentable ignorance of all things nautical which was only equalled by her enthusiasm to be on the sea. One sailorly thing we did, and that was to catch the tide below the weir at exactly the right moment, and on it we were carried gracefully past Sharpham Woods.

Few landowners can have chosen their site so happily

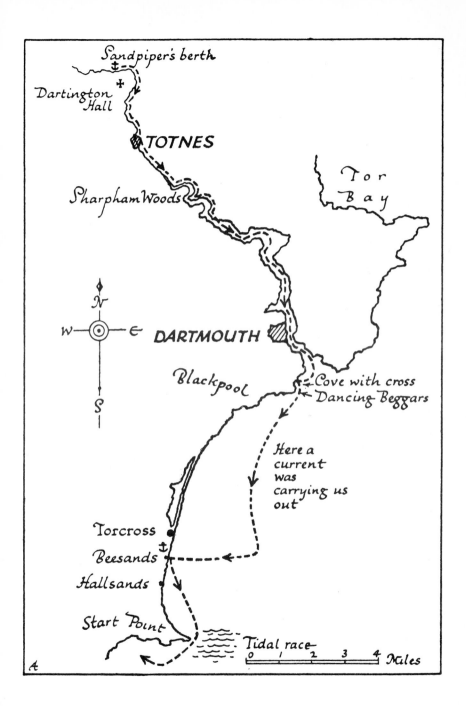

for beauty, sunshine, health and peace as did the old squires of Sharpham. The big mansion stands sufficiently elevated on a ridge between two arms of the river.

On one side the parkland is bounded by the glorious woods of the steep riverside and on the other by the high ramparts of the Tuckenhay plateau. And now the woods from Sharpham to Stoke Gabriel and Dittisham were beginning to get afire with points of green light - the buds and leaves of spring; so enchanting were these glades that nothing but the old mysterious murmur of the sea could have called us away from them.

Past awakening farmsteads we went, past the blossoming orchards of Dittisham, past the moored hulks of pensioned ships, until at Dartmouth we met the vigorous life of shipping and the traffic of the sea. In less than an hour from Totnes we passed between the castles, out to the blue and the burnished gold of a calm, sunbathed sea.

Sandpiper immediately turned her nose southward, as if she knew of fair coasts awaiting her, and we paddled on by cliffs and lofty hillsides of a wild loveliness.

A mile further our attention was caught by a white cross gleaming on the cliff face of a small, inaccessible cove. Jean's curiosity and my desire for a respite from being knocked on the head by her paddle combined to bring us swiftly to the shore. We found the strange object to be a marble cross to the memory of one Christopher Reade, I believe, who fell from the cliff above and whose dying words, "It's all right", were recorded on this stone. Perhaps these are meaningless, automatic words of a semi-conscious man or perhaps, uttered at this shrine of rare beauty, they express the profoundest philosophy of life and death.

We were somewhat silent for a time but soon, such is the unteachable self-confidence of man, I conceived a desire to climb the cliff to get a photograph of the cove. I considered sufficient respect was paid to the gruesome reminder on the cliff face if I climbed the opposite wall. Having got my photograph I began the descent but on a scree my foot slipped and I came bounding down. Somehow I managed to avoid a direct hit from the jagged rocks and even kept the camera safely clutched in my hand, but at the bottom of the scree, just as I was coming to rest, a veritable spear of rock more cunning or malevolent than the rest penetrated my guard and stabbed me in the small of the back. The camera crashed on the beach, which is why the photographs of this part, ruined by light fogging, are even worse than the others.

For myself, I tottered to the boat, but my paddling, in virtue of my bruised spine, was even more erratic than Jean's and I knew we shouldn't get much further that day.

In this fashion we reached Combe Point and passed through an archipelago of jagged rock pinnacles slanting out of the water at crazy angles. They are called the Dancing Beggars and very drolly do they suggest a

group of dancing, tattered humans. Not content with
the recent experience I climbed on one of these to
photograph Jean amidst them. We were both somewhat
nervous, however, Jean because it was the first time
she had been left to manage a boat alone and I because
if she failed to get me aboard again I was doomed to
spend the rest of my days sitting on a very spiky
dancing beggar. Fishermen who meet the Dancing Beggars
in bad light and with an onshore wind are apt to mis-
pronounce their title, I am told.

At Combe Point one is rewarded by bursting upon a
magnificent view of Start Bay. The four mile stretch of
curving beach, of a curious coarse sand, has the yel-
lowish gold shade of a Cornish cove, a shade unusual
among the richer sandstone sands of Devon. Before
Slapton beach came the strangely shining shale cliffs
of Little Dartmouth, the colour of a purple pansy,
preceded by the coves of Blackpool and Stoke Fleming.
Beyond lay the black mass of Start Point with the
warning finger of its lighthouse, making us acutely
aware of being out in the open space of the Channel.

Off Blackpool we hoisted sail to a tiny breeze. There
lies one of the finest jewels of all that are strung
along the coast of South Devon. In its rare seclusion,

66

its freedom from the builder, its beautifully proportioned natural beauty, it is the complete antithesis of its namesake in the north. At this time of the year it is at its loveliest, and not a single footmark marred the clean sweep of its beach.

There must be some current here which sets strongly out to sea, for after an hour's idling with a truant wind, we found ourselves quite two miles out. Once more the galley slaves were set to the paddles and we made a course for Torcross, enjoying nevertheless the finer view which our remoteness from the shore gave us.

About this time I took a compass bearing on the lone hotel in the middle of Slapton Sands, that hotel beloved of fishermen who come to the quiet, reed-edged waters of Slapton Ley.

The golden sickle of Start Bay all too often reaps a harvest of wreckage. In 1873 a large Shanghai clipper strewed 1300 tons of tea and 60 tons of tobacco along the shore "in ridges eleven feet high". At the moment it is covered, more prosaically and certainly less comfortably, by tons of scrap iron from a wrecked Belgian steamer.

Our course here was certainly very peculiar, for whereas we were heading for Torcross our movement was out past the Start Lighthouse - a proceeding which Jean, in her ignorance, imputed to uneven paddling but which I could only credit to some devilish current aided by the wind which now blew straight at us from Torcross. Torcross is, up to the time of writing, a picturesque, tiny fishing village, having a footing precariously between the wide sea and the waters of the Ley, keeping one end of itself tacked to the southern cliffs for security. In the highest easterly gales the waves wash around the steps of the yellow stuccoed cottages, which are mostly caulked with tar and pitch like the long boats lying beside them on the beach.

Beesands, now on our port bow and about two miles south of Torcross retains, by virtue of bad roads, the simplicity which Torcross is about to lose. It remains essentially a little community of fishermen, clinging to a difficult coast and forcing a meagre livelihood from a cruel sea. For them the word community has its full meaning. Indeed many of the fishing villages of the west are primitive communist experiments, and nowhere have I seen this so well developed as at Beesands and perhaps Beer. The children, like the children of Plato's *Republic*, seem to belong to everyone and to go in and out of any house. The hens and chickens do likewise, bestowing eggs wherever the spirit moves them.

Valuable fishing gear, crab pots and essential stores are left all over the beach. When the boats - mostly motorboats nowadays - have to be hauled out of the water, all able-bodied inhabitants turn to man the capstans, no matter whose boat is coming ashore; and if any man lose his nets at sea it is taken for granted that the community will share his loss.

Domestic washing is strung all over the beach, often on the rigging of boats about to go to sea. Cats feed contentedly on the morning's catch of fish, whilst ducks, making their nests under the ship's tiller, have to be driven out before the men can go a-fishing. Harper, whose perceptions of Devon are always acute, says, "There is something Irish in the look, the manners and the customs of Beesands."

Until a few years ago Beesands consisted only of a picturesque, tide-line of cottages, but, perhaps warned by the disaster which befell the neighbouring village of Hallsands, the recent builders have retreated a bit inland, unfortunately adopting a brick "council house" mode of construction.

Never, I think, could Beesands fishermen have come so wearily to shore as we did then. For the mysterious drift had brought us almost opposite Beesands, and we were heading straight for the beach as if we had come across the Channel. Yonder was the soft sweep of the beach with its suggestion of reclining at ease. But before us a stretch of ruffled blue water which seemed unending and into which our aching arms dipped paddles in vain. I fixed my eyes on a heap of stones in front of two isolated cottages and determined not to take them off until our keel grated on the pebbles. At least, I thought it was a heap of stones, but presently, when I lay beside it on the beach, recovering, it said, "Du'ee comm very var in 'ee?" and opening my eyes I found myself regarding a very ancient man sitting on a tub. His face had what I can only describe as the typical expression of the old Devon rustic, kindly and sociable - yet still strong and independent. It was like a very wrinkled apple with the colours of summer still shining through and lit by two shrewd, jovial, blue eyes. They were not the stern, hawk-like eyes of the fisherman, hardened by much wary watching of the treacherous immensity of the sea; indeed, I gathered that this man was surveying the sea, merely because he wanted to have his back to his work - the land.

My guess proved correct; for soon the ancient was talking about his son's farm, which ran inland from this point.

We camped very agreeably on the wide expanse of turf behind the foreshore which no man seemed to claim. Though it was only May the night never became very cold. Next morning, turning to the beach we found the ancient, good as his word, sitting in the morning sunlight keeping watch on *Sandpiper*.

It was a lovely morning, with a slight swell breaking on the beach. The difficulty in launching a boat depends as much on the beach as on the swell. Where a pebble beach runs steeply into deep water, as here, the waves do not come in open formation with a formal sequence of mounting breaker, crashing wave, broken wave and crawling foam. Instead, one's troubles, as Shakespeare pointed out in another connection, come all together. The waves constitute a continuous barrage of direct hammer blows upon the beach; it is all rampant waves, rebounding spray and screaming shingle.

Twice we rushed the barrage and twice *Sandpiper* buried her nose like a submarine. With that we became ingenious and tried launching the boat sideways, a proceeding which involved our getting wet to our waists - and in what month is the sea colder than in May! We lifted her over the breaking wave and paused to climb aboard. And in that instant a more cunning wave than the others opened its jaws a little wider and smashed poor *Sandpiper* upon the beach, shattering the coaming joints and drenching everything.

Boisterously the bubbling water laughed at our discomfiture, but, faced with the task of rounding the Start, I was in no mood for such a send-off, and I thought very sympathetically of that Emperor Xerxes who had the tide of the Bosphorus lashed with chains for washing away his bridge of boats.

Whilst watching our garments spread out to dry I became aware of the ancient unobtrusively at my elbow. Doubtless he had seen far worse wrecks upon the beach.

"The zee be vair wicked yeer," he said. "Do'ee go and 'ave a luke at Hallsands yonder to zee what un can do when un be prapper wild." Very tactful that, I thought.

"I'll kape me eye on these yeer things fur 'ee," he assured us. So we clambered a mile towards the Start to view the astounding sight of ocean-battered Hallsands.

These strange ruins tell a touching story of human love, courage and stupidity. The fishermen built their homes beside their boats, clinging to the foot of the cliff, with only a narrow shingle beach between themselves and the hungry sea. On winter nights the storms would send the surf to the doors of the houses. One writer speaks of "foolhardihood that induced mortal man to build houses in this perilous position", but these men rightly loved to live in the sunlight and the spray, next to the element they served and understood. It was government contractors, more pitiless than the sea, removing, in spite of protests, thousands of tons of limestone shingle from this beach, who were, in fact, responsible for the catastrophe.

In the stout wall and the intersecting ramparts before these ruined houses you can see how this little village tried valiantly to defend itself against the storms which each year came further than any man had known. But no one moved. Conservative impulses have always withstood the plain indications of reason. We are told that the landlady of the inn was serving tea (probably expressing her views on scaremongers) when

Hallsands intact

the side of the house fell out. The onshore gale and
spring tides wiped out the whole village in a couple of
days. You will find only a number of broken walls and
fallen roofs, looking exactly like a derelict war village blasted by a deluge of shell.

After regarding so monstrous a disaster we found
ourselves looking at *Sandpiper* without any sense of
ill-luck. Nevertheless she could not be launched that
day and, once postponed, our attack on the Start was
not to be realised until June. Arriving at Beesands in
that benign month we found nothing altered but the sea.
The ancient, utterly unchanged, was still valiantly
keeping his back turned upon work. He told us how the
fishermen on this long beach once trained Newfoundland
dogs to swim through the surf to bring the ropes ashore
from incoming boats so that the latter could be hauled
swiftly up on the beach. Evidently there were brains in
these parts once.

The day was a lovely one, and we needed it, for we
hoped to pass two landmarks - crucial danger points -

namely, Start Point and Prawle Point. The ancient, who seemed to have got attached to us, watched our preparations for departure with what looked suspiciously like a tear in his bright blue eye. He had misgivings.

"I wunna try to go round the Staart in that li'l boaat! Tees vair zilly for zhure. You'me gwain to be drownded prapper."

Finding us set in our strange refusal to face old age, he called his missus from the cottage to relate all the drownings on the coast (she having a better memory than he). Unfortunately for his plans of dissuasion the missus became very intrigued with the boat, the provisioning, and indeed with the whole plan. For two pins she would have accompanied us. (Are old women more adventurous than old men?) We waved good-bye to the lovely old couple, leaving them furnished with a subject of discussion for the day, and set a straight course for the Start Lighthouse.

For all sailors in tiny craft - and even in big ones, as I have heard a cruiser gunner declare - the rounding of the Start is an experience in itself. For us it was also an achievement, equivalent to a big vessel's rounding of the Horn. For it is the haunt of a fierce tidal race, which in rough weather spreads a dread regiment of enormous white horses two or three miles out to sea. Even in the calmest weather the surface of the sea is twisted and tortured as by a far-flung whirlpool and from which the maddest whisperings and groanings rise into the still air. Sailors swear that the spirits of drowned seamen meet here. If so they must be expiating a peculiarly wicked life. Perhaps among them is that "Henri Muge, a pirate of the sea" who, according to local records, was hanged upon Start Point for all sailors to behold.

To make a detour around the race, far out to sea, did not appeal to me; better to try to slip past near the shore and risk the rocks. Then I told Jean what to expect. It was well that I did, for even so she confesses her heart sank at the sight of the first long whale-backed roller that rushed at us. It was incredible to see these rollers rise out of a dead-calm, oily sea. They came at us with a curious sideways motion, feinting like a boxer. Jean looked longingly at the little lane that runs round the firm cliff-side to the dignified white lighthouse, and remarked with some relief that a coastguard was watching our progress with an interested eye. For a few minutes we had an exhilarating tussle - no roller actually broke in our vicinity - and, owing to our clinging to the coast we were soon out of it.

The Start was passed! Its massive outline, built in hard gneiss rock and shining quartz, serrated like the scaly back of some prehistoric monster, closed the view behind us. Before us was the almost equally rugged Peartree Point - a windswept waste on which I am sure no pear tree would ever consent to grow.

On passing this, a view of extreme loveliness presented itself. In the wide bay that runs round to Prawle Point there is at first not a sign of human habitation. A tiny plaything of a cliff skirts the water, and behind this comes a curious flat terrace of greensward and bracken - ideal for picnicking, camping or cricket - which rises into a second and very lofty cliff-face nearly a quarter of a mile from the water. This cliff is now softened in most parts into a steep gorse-grown slope from which huge shoulders of naked rock - like tors upon the moor - project at intervals. Presumably this was once a sea cliff. This peculiar formation is called "The Narrows", and a very lovely picture it makes.

At intervals we saw tiny coves in the low cliff glowing golden in the morning sunlight, and closer inspection shewed an occasional fisherman's cottage tucked in a gully with long boats drawn up on the sands. One of the loveliest of these coves is Lannacombe, accessible from the South Hams by an atrociously narrow and bumpy lane, not bad enough alas, to prevent, in recent years, quite a row of cars collecting there in the month of August.

In the far distance, against the skyline, we saw the little cluster of buildings that marks Prawle village. Harper aptly describes East Prawle as arrested "in the act of developing from a farmyard to a village". Considering that it aspires to be a fishing village and yet is perched on a hill half a morning's climb from the sea, this arrest is not surprising. Still, the situation of Prawle is as uniquely beautiful as its isolation is splendid, and I have seen framed in its cottage doorways, great square-shouldered men with curling golden hair and rugged faces, noble as those of Greek gods.

Since rounding the Start the second mate had been taking a much more rosy view of life. Indeed, inflated by her promotion to the ranks of the experienced mariners, she had been singing for the past five minutes "Over the sea to Skye": a delightful lilt to go with the rhythm of paddling on this gently heaving sea. But now, glimpsing those jewelled coves, she dropped her paddle with the gesture of a revolting galley slave and demanded to go ashore that we might explore one. Always it was the second mate who cried "Let us linger and enjoy the present" and I, the navigator, who urged the necessity of paying regard to the realities of tide and wind and of keeping schedule. "We must reach the shelter of Kingsbridge estuary while the weather is good," I argued. "We will come back to these beauty spots when we have explored the whole coast."

But, as in life, there is no coming back. Either one never gets the opportunity again, or, if one does, it is not the same - the delight of novelty is gone; the light has changed. So, fellow navigator, knowing what I tell you here of the whole coast, forget schedules, tides or winds, and enjoy the eternal present in whatever lovely spot you may find upon such a calm and golden morning.

Chapter 6

In Deepest South Devon

Prawle Point, the arm of Devon thrusting itself farthest south into the open spaces of the Channel, was
marked on my chart as a danger point which we might
never weather, for it is Prawle rather than Start which
catches the full force of the south-westerly gales. It
held significance also as a milestone marking the half-
way point of our journey, and as a corner round which
we should suddenly come upon an entirely novel and
unfrequented stretch of coast.

Now it lay before us, like a great stone lion de-
fending the southernmost gateway of the county. Yet
this rounding of the cape was a very different business
from what it might have been. I had imagined us waiting for days or weeks in the lee of the headland until
the sou'wester should momentarily call off the legions
of breakers which it continually flings against this
bastion. I had been preparing myself for the most
critical battle of the voyage, against waves almost too
big for *Sandpiper* to face. I had pictured us wet to
the skin, straining for hours with creaking timbers and
miles of unscalable cliffs frowning before and behind
us.

Lo, the almost imperceptible swell on the great burnished mirror of the Channel had departed, leaving it
as quiet as a lily pond. The huge grey rocks, admittedly, looked unscalable, but they slept like good-

natured giants in the noonday sun. Even the sea-gulls only nodded and croaked drowsily as we passed.

Farthest South! The horizon had melted and the pale azure sea passed without a break into a hazy azure sky. This was Devon shewing its tropical blood. We sprawled on our paddles, gazing enviously at the velvet blackness of the fantastic shadows in the natural flying buttress at the cliff-end. A flash of sunlight from the cliff-top told us that the lone coastguard was busy with his telescope. Days afterwards, when I walked back to this station, I found in charge a man who had been with Scott's "Farthest South" expedition to the South Pole. When he sat at Devon's 'farthest south' on sweltering summer days, idly recording the passage of distant ships shimmering in the heat, did he have visions of blue walls of glistening ice and great snowfields untrodden by mortal man?

I say 'idly', but it is no idle task to record the ships that pass Prawle Point. Half the liners, tramp steamers, barges and fishing trawlers that use the corridor of the English Channel pass by that window; and if you are a connoisseur of ships you may spend a very interesting day there armed with a sufficiently powerful telescope.

Now the very varnish of our coaming began to blister

in the torrid heat. Heat like this saps the spirit. It will shrivel your ambitions, wilt your ideals and evaporate your very dreams to an empty haze. I have lived with Germans in the bracing cold of East Prussia, and felt like them - a being of lively will and iron determination. And I have seen these same friends, brought into a Devonshire summer, reduced to pitiable jellyfish, devoid of the spirit of a common vegetable.

It is not roast beef, nor cider, nor Devonshire cream which is responsible for empire builders, but climate; for the men who could shew sufficient enterprise to man and victual a ship in this climate are bound to shine as paragons of will and determination when they arrive in any other climate of the world.

Presently our determined slogging at the paddles was rewarded by as fair a sight as one may meet along all the south coast: Salcombe, nestling in the wooded recesses of the estuary, guarded by the bold sentinel rocks of Bolt Head. Eyeing the four-mile stretch of water ahead I calculated that we should reach the bar in perfect time for the inward tide.

But I had counted without the second mate, who had sighted on the starboard bow "a perfectly heavenly little beach". It was so lovely a cove that, even without the dire threat of mutiny, I was prepared to take *Sandpiper* to shore.

The man who called it Black Cove must assuredly have been sprinkling names on a map without looking at the places themselves, or perhaps he was thinking of those two proud Spanish galleons which dashed themselves to pieces on the citadel-like Gammon Head which forms an arm around the cove. Their gallant crews sleep well in so sweet a resting place.

From the sea it is like a golden blossom set shyly in a hedge of thorns. Doubly attractive it was to us then, by reason of the pools of black shadow beneath the high cliffs. As we weary wanderers floated idly in over the pellucid green water the sea-gulls rose in protesting white clouds. In a cool, sandy sea cave we dropped asleep, forgetting the clamour of the gulls and the merciless heat of the sun.

In high summer, Black Cove is the haunt of a few yachtsmen from Salcombe. And here again the law is exemplified that the farther afield you go the nicer are the holidaymakers you will find. There is a sieving and sorting by distance, by taste and the arduousness of the journey to beauty. The range of humanity from Southend to Salcombe is very great, and I say this in no spirit of snobbery but in love of the standards that make Salcombe.

Out of Black Cove we paddled over waters as clear as crystal, feeling more like an airship than a boat. On the gentle green carpet of the shoulders of the hills around the estuary entrance the gorse glowed like scattered embers of wind-blown fire. An hour's paddling brings us opposite Bull Rocks - perhaps so called because they roar in face of the south-west gales, and now we begin to feel the gentle grip of the tide which was to bear us up the estuary.

On either side the little bays and golden sands of Salcombe beckon. Where is there sand of a lovelier, livelier hue than this? Wondrously they beckon to the sea-weary mariner and to add glamour to their call they are sprinkled in summer with sprawling sirens in many-coloured bathing costumes.

Through the limpid pale green waters we can clearly see the yellow sand of the bar, eight feet, six feet, and now four feet beneath our keel. As it shallows we see the rocky islands, marked by lantern poles - the molars which grind the victims caught by the fangs of the bar. For though we drift lazily now, lulled to languor by the pleasant sights and sounds, Salcombe can present a very different aspect to the sailor. I have seen the beauty of its other face in winter, when the gale thunders harshly through the dripping, straining pine woods and howls furiously against the black buttresses of Bolt Head. Then the bar is a death-trap for any homing sailor and all too many have come to grief there. It stretches - a white line of raging waters - from the eastern bank to within a stone's throw of the high western cliff, leaving the narrowest of safe passages, and it may well be called the most dangerous bar

on the south coast. Even in summer there are many yachtsmen who will not dare to enter after dark, and since the tide may be unsuitable during the day it is something of a feat to get into Salcombe, a feat which so exhausts some that, once accomplished, they drop anchor and go ashore for the rest of the season!

We are in full sight now of the clustering houses and white river-side hotels of Salcombe, on our port bow, and of the high green hills of Portlemouth to starboard. Why is it that in South Devon estuaries the town always springs up on the right bank leaving the left deserted? Perhaps they shelter thus from the southwester: I can think of no other cause for this phenomenon.

By some miracle of mercy, Salcombe, in spite of its incomparable natural beauty, has remained one of the few completely unspoilt gems of Devon. Its compact little streets are neat and clean but quaintly old-fashioned, its tasteful villas are in lovely grounds where every kind of tree seems to flourish. If it must spawn characterless terraces it chooses to do so over the hill away from the river.

So it remains a haunt of yachtsmen, whose proud craft make a brave sight in the pool of the estuary; a home of cherished natural beauty for landsmen of good taste and a summer resort for visitors who love it as it is and who make it populous without making it at all vulgar.

Many years ago Salcombe decided by a majority vote that it didn't want the railway. Elsewhere the shop and hotel-keepers by sheer numbers might have defeated such a resolution; for in some places no moral odium attaches to putting bank balances before the beauty and integrity of the homeland. But these were wiser men and their policy of seclusion has justified itself up to the hilt.

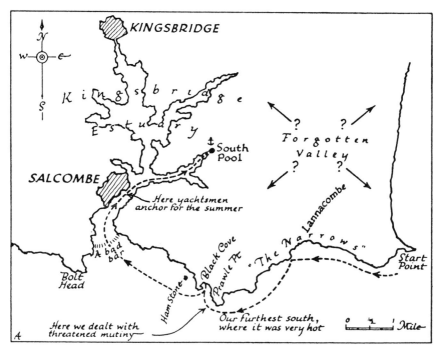

Although Salcombe is a bride of the sea, if ever there was one, it can also offer some magnificent walking country. Around Bolt Head and extending to Hope Cove is one of the finest cliff walks to be found in England. It is now preserved by the National Trust after a tussle with some local landowner, a fight sustained by public heroes who are unknown. One should climb also past Portlemouth and by Bolberry and Mal-

80

borough. The church of the latter is of unusual size and design and has a slender steeple which is a landmark far and wide, indeed, few ships would navigate these parts without its pilotage. In the churchyard a simple stone records the loss of a son of Malborough in one of the first and pioneer submarines - a reminder, this, of the tribute which the sea and the glory of our naval history has exacted from all Devon villages. A far journey it must have seemed from the open sunny street of this lofty village to the dark, dank prison of a sunken submarine.

We have lost sight of Malborough steeple, for the swift tide bears us round into deep-walled South Pool creek, and now we lose sight of Salcombe too: it is suddenly swallowed up by the wooded hills and we are instantly in a world of complete rural seclusion. Henceforth we belong to the land, not to the sea. We landed in the woods to have tea and for this purpose we took ashore an extremely patent oil vapour stove purchased by Jean and which had lain unused in *Sandpiper* ever since we left Totnes. It burnt petrol, and on that account I had steadfastly refused to light it in the boat, being convinced by the evil smile on its brassy face, that it intended at once to blow us, and *Sandpiper* to smithereens. Baulked in this intention by being taken ashore, it cunningly permitted itself to light quietly, in the hope of deceiving us, but, resenting a second kettle, it burned furiously (like an oxyacetylene burner) and melted the bottom out of our kettle, so it was ignominiously stowed away again in the hold.

Whither are we bound now? Though I have disclosed all other ports of call I must beg the privilege of keeping this a secret. We are going to Joan's cottage which lies in what I will call the Forgotten Valley, since, despite its being one of the loveliest little valleys in South Devon, it is forgotten by visitors, and indeed by most Devon folk themselves, even in the height of summer. This much of the secret I will disclose: that it lies an hour's walk over the hills from the tidal limit of South Pool creek. So we float between the spreading trees towards South Pool.

That old cobb-walled cottage has welcomed in many homing mariners. Apparently far inland it might yet be called a yachtsman's rendezvous. I am reminded particularly of the party that came home from a moonlight sail, planned at the cottage during a hot breathless day, when the cool waters under the harvest moon beckoned to all with irresistible appeal.

But if I may presume to give advice on so delicate a subject as a moonlight sailing party, let me warn you to summon up all your will-power and eschew it as you would a lunatic asylum - which indeed it is. On such parties I have seen strong men reduced to wiping tears from their eyes with the jib-boom and women of grace and charm striking each other on the head with the tiller.

I know the blandishments, indeed the magic, of the occasion. One wakes, as it were, from the stuporous heat of a long and dusty summer day, to a new dawn of purple twilight. One's spirits gather fresh life in the cool, refreshing breeze of evening which sends awakening ripples shivering across a sea long petrified in a hot, oily calm. A red-gold harvest moon, of enormous roundness, throws across the shifting, fantastic colours of the ocean a trail of purest splendour, a magic carpet leading out to the horizon - to hidden lands of high romance. There is adventure in the night; a promise of magic in the breeze which strokes one's hair; a spell in the hazy shadows of the coast. What youths or maidens would be so foolish as to resist the ineffable melody which calls them to hoist the silver sail and steal in a ghostly ship out of the harbour, over the dark, purple sea?

But let me tell my tale. There was Joan's lovely new boat, and seven eager people packing tins and ruck-sacks, in a spirit of infectious adventurousness, for the night's cruise. On my refusing to be the eighth member, I was at first regarded kindly as a sick person needing an aspirin, and later as a ridiculous lunatic. I was sorry, for it was an ill-assorted crew needing another sailor; but did not the moon deliberately wink at me around the thatched roof of the cottage?

However, they left in high spirits and hoisted sails to a steady breeze from the sea, which lifted a gentle swell. Reports of what happened are necessarily con-flicting, for the truth is not readily divulged to one who looked, even if he did not say, "I told you so." Apparently someone had thrown the three rucksacks into the boat from the quayside. Consequently, after an hour, when everyone was feeling a bit cold and asking for hot coffee, the thermos flasks were opened one by one revealing in each and every case the same sad story of broken glass. Joan, as the skipper and a bit of a martinet at that, started an inquisition, which Donald Swan said was superfluous since the coffee was already spilt. This argument only brought down upon him the general suspicion that he was the culprit, and he retired to the foot of the mast in some disgrace, ostracised from good society.

Nor were matters improved by Donald mentioning food. As he might have seen in a better light, every face had the look of preoccupation which comes of what religious people call an 'inner experience' but which in this case was a by-product of a rising swell. Every roll of the boat brought the smell of bilge water, mingled with the coffee which it now contained, and with this reminder of Donald's criminal negligence fresh in their nostrils the others now gave him such hard looks that he confesses to coming near to throwing himself overboard. Nothing but the thought of four bottles of 'perry', which he and Huggins had hidden by the mast, prevented him from doing so.

Jennifer was the first to give a forfeit to Neptune, after which she felt much better. Indeed, soon she felt so hungry that she joined Donald in a renewed cry for food. The mention of this subject had alarming effects on those who up till now had prolonged the inner struggle, and while they were leaning over the side, supposedly to enjoy the moonlight, Donald and Huggins made short work of the bottles of perry.

After that there was a general desertion of the posts of duty. Everyone was feeling intensely cold, but unfortunately, in a boat of that size, there was only room for one person to lie down comfortably, and there were seven candidates for the position. Joan had high words with Maisie, the first mate, over some matter of navigation - not that anyone was really bothering any more about where the boat might go - and Maisie determinedly went to sleep on the anchor in the bow. Huggins complacently stretched himself for slumber in the only clear space, constituting himself an obstacle to all control of the sails and a general peril to the navigation of the boat.

Hard words were said to Huggins, but a man who can sleep on two brass rowlocks and a zinc baler, and pillow his head on a hard-wood block, is not easily moved by words. No one mentioned the moon any more. It had lost its harvest-moon magic, having climbed high into the sky to become a hard, expressionless, chromium button. And with that, the landscape lost its ethereal beauty, becoming just a badly-lit smudge abutting on a monotonous, endlessly-corrugated sea. As the gilt wore off the moon so the disillusioned crew began to wrangle with each other and with the skipper - indeed it was

84

the only way to keep warm. Only Huggins and Donald slumbered on, to the mystification of everyone – for the bottles of perry had not been seen – and to the intense irritation of those less comfortably placed.

The official narrative gets hazy here because the narrator was fast asleep and the other evidence is conflicting, but apparently at about two o'clock in the morning a general mutiny broke out and the boat was put about for harbour with a very strained atmosphere between the captain and the crew.

Indeed, the captain steered with her nose so much in the air (according to the crew) that she completely failed to see the yacht *Hope* moored full in her path. *Hope's* bowsprit suddenly appeared over the bows, tore into the mainsail near the mast, split it from end to end and then caught in the stays. Instantly all was confusion. Frozen and half asleep, everyone leapt up (except Huggins) to do the heroic thing.

A moment's inspection convinced Donald that the boats could only be separated, if at all, by someone climbing on to *Hope's* bowsprit, so he proceeded to do this. He was, he says, befuddled with sleep, but it is not certain whether this is meant to explain his valour or his subsequent thoughtlessness. At any rate, when he had successfully disconnected the boats he forgot to disconnect himself from the bowsprit, so that his own boat drifted away leaving him dangling in mid-air. Drifted is perhaps hardly the word, for she went down wind among the other yachts at a great rate with flapping sail fragments and in a general state of chaos. As for Donald, his cries growing fainter and fainter in the distance, faded out of the crew's thoughts altogether in view of the – for them – more urgent problems now confronting them. Somehow they lowered the sails and got out oars, but – horror of horrors – no one could find the rowlocks! In this condition they ran against an immaculate motor-yacht resplendent in white enamel. Now that very afternoon I had been near this yacht and had lifted a boat-hook to fend off. The moment I did so an excitable little man leapt out of the cabin and pranced up and down the deck in a fit of hysterics, forbidding me to touch his beautiful enamel or indeed any part of his beautiful boat in any spot whatever.

In the contingency which had now occurred he promised well to lose more than the enamel! Doubtless this was the eventuality that had been giving him sleepless nights. At any rate, he shot up from below in a split second, wearing a peaked cap and a nightgown (so Maisie vows). Possibly he thought the hideous spectacle and the still more hideous noise were part of a dreadful nightmare, but he swore ferociously for all that.

Indeed, so appalling was the language that even Huggins woke up and straightway reproached the man for using such terms in a public thoroughfare and before ladies. The enemy's reply was to throw a bucket of bilge water over Huggins and Huggins thereupon threw most of the uneaten supper, including several tomatoes, over the man, his boat and his enamel.

Huggins' rising from his bed, of course, revealed the missing rowlocks, and with their aid the contending parties were withdrawn to a safe distance. Rowing slowly up wind, listening for the guiding bleat of Donald's piteous appeals, the crew at length rediscovered him, still clinging to the bowsprit of *Hope* with incomparable devotion.

This reunion, it seems, was a very touching one, for Donald shewed intense joy at seeing them, which was more than anyone else had done that night, and they were deeply moved.

The return of that mutinous rabble to the cottage at five o'clock in the morning awakened me from delicious slumbers. Or rather I was not awakened by the rabble itself, which was strangely and ominously silent, but by the scornful trumpet note with which the cockerel greeted their appearance. I opened one eye just enough to see the waning moon throw me a portentous wink before it tucked itself below the horizon.

Two hours later I came downstairs to a scene resembling a stricken battlefield. They lay in ungainly heaps just as sleep had struck them down, with their gear sprawling beside them where they fell. Only the

skipper had had the indomitable will to tack upstairs
in face of the headwinds of exhaustion. She had dropped
anchor on her truckle bed and I could see by the determined set of her chin, and the defiant fling of the
black curls, that even in sleep she was still steering
seawards in face of a mutinous and incompetent lower
deck.

Fortunately there is a strange alchemy about the air
of the Forgotten Valley which distils away all peevish
thoughts imported from the outer world, so that when
the party gathered for lunch no merrier shipmates could
be imagined. How everyone laughed, not least the skipper, at the comic nightmare, begotten of moonlight,
which all had dreamed the night before! But I enjoyed
the story most of all, being fresh from a good night's
rest.

It was dusk when Jean and I floated up to the
thatched white cottages of South Pool and commenced our
climb through the deep-set lanes, among flitting bats
and the drowsy flight of moths. Glow-worms delighted
our eyes with green Chinese lanterns in the hedges, but
the night was very close and we were so heavy with
sleep as to appreciate above all the warm glow of the
lighted casement window of the cottage.

Once we lost the way, for there are few places harder
to find than the Forgotten Valley, which is ingeniously
surrounded by a Hampton Court maze of narrow lanes, all
designed to lead away. Indeed, friends visiting us by
car, even with the most precise instructions or after
previous visits, seldom arrive without the help of a
search party. At three o'clock the familiar horn is
heard as they approach from the north; at half-past
three they are again heard tootling valiantly half a
mile way in eastern marches; at four a forlorn hooting
floats over the hill from the south-west. Then we send
out a search party and bring them in to tea.

No search party was needed that night, for soon we
heard music floating through the warm dusk, and in a
moment friends were welcoming the weary mariners in. I
remained awake long enough to write the log for the
day, by the gentle light of watching candles, but soon,

in the slumbrous air of the Forgotten Valley, I had forgotten the weariness of the long pull into Salcombe, the sinister tidal waves of the Start and the burning glare by the sun-scorched rocks of Prawle.

Chapter 7

The Kingsbridge Estuary

Any small-boat sailor could spend a whole season very happily amidst the tidal creeks and lake-like expanses of the Kingsbridge estuary. Indeed, we very nearly did so, for the fortnight we had planned fled so quickly that we delayed in getting out to sea again. In that delay a south-westerly gale blew up which locked the door to the sea for another three weeks.

You may idle in wooded bays and creeks like that of South Pool, and visit pretty waterside villages like Frogmore, tucked away at the ends of creeks. You may enjoy the morning in the colourful seaside sports of Salcombe, and float up with the tide to spend the evening wandering in old-world Kingsbridge at the head of the estuary. There is a cultured, park-like quality in much of the Kingsbridge estuary and a complete absence either of the rugged grandeur of the adjoining coast or of the mysterious jungles of the Dart and Erme. One passes lovely estates that are evidently the pride and joy of some kinglet of these quiet valleys, so trim and neat are the farms, so artistically attuned are the materials and the style of the manor house and its dependent cottages.

An especially fine settlement we passed on the following day as we dropped down the curving waters of South Pool creek to paddle with the high tide up the main estuary towards Kingsbridge. The houses of Kingsbridge, seen from the estuary, seem curiously to be craning their necks over one another's shoulders in an attempt to see what is coming up the river.

Kingsbridge and Dodbrook, which insist on being distinct towns, although all their streets interlace, constitute an old market town with a decent sense of quiet prosperity and offering occasional glimpses of "high life" when the gentry from the neighbouring estates "come to town". Kingsbridge is famed in history for a drink, "white ale", which some say is still made here, but I have never been able to get a taste of it; fortunately, the old stagers say, for it apparently contained among other things, eggs, pepper and spices, milk and gin. It was evidently the aboriginal cocktail. Wise old men tell me that it accounts for the great age of Devonians in these parts: the man whose constitution can stand one gulp has nothing more to fear from the ravages of time. Two generations ago Kingsbridge had a thriving trade, engaging about one hundred and fifty vessels with the Mediterranean, and possibly the drink is a hybrid of the drinks of northern and southern climes.

At Kingsbridge, wonder of wonders to relate, we found the old first mate waiting for us on the quay. *Sandpiper* and the skipper were glad to take her aboard again for what proved to be the last trip with which she honoured the seas of these parts. A little enquiry, however, revealed the fact that her desire to go to sea for the day was partly due to a certain embarrassment at staying in Kingsbridge. It appears that, as a teacher, her independent manners had given some uneasy moments to the elders of the town. In particular, she had been given to shewing her incomparable legs about the town in a pair of diminutive tennis shorts. This was not considered good education, for, said the committee, did not experience with chorus girls shew that women with good legs could not possibly have good minds?

So, poor girl, she had to go to sea once more to give Kingsbridge time to recover its sense of perspective. Into all manner of strange creeks we sailed, and landed for lunch on a fair round hill, left practically an island, between the Dodbrooke and the Frogmore Creeks. An essential part of the scenery in the upper arms of the estuary are the numerous tiny castles set in the miniature wooded cliffs flanking the water. On closer examination these proved to be round, stone limekilns but they are none the less romantic spots for picnicking for all that.

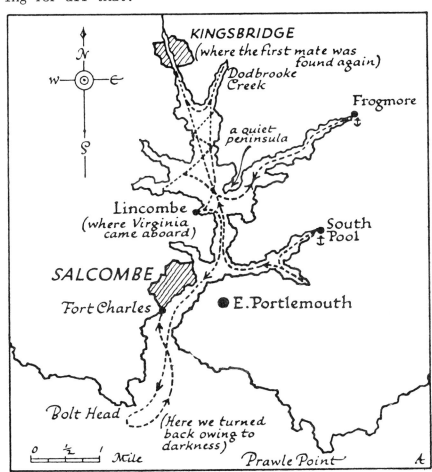

How warm the estuary is for bathing! I doubt if there is warmer water anywhere on the south coast than in this shallow sun bowl. We intended to explore Frogmore

Creek; but we had our bathe before turning upstream again, since the banks get muddy higher up. So we sailed placidly up to Frogmore itself which, with the wide pool of vagrant sea-water lapping around its little bridge and the sunlight on its whitewashed cottages, is a very agreeable Devonshire Venice. Unfortunately, after tea in the Globe, which was served by one of Monica's pupils, whose delighted face was wreathed in smiles, we returned to find the creek as dry as the main road; so quickly does the tide come in and run out in these upper reaches!

Sandpiper was ignominiously lifted over a hedge and placed in a cottage garden under the care of an old farm labourer who guaranteed its safety. Nevertheless next day we had to remove two hens, a garden shovel and a bucket of hogwash from *Sandpiper's* outraged interior, before setting her on the tide.

Nowhere in the British Isles will you find so near an approach to genuinely subtropical vegetation as in these deep sheltered valleys of southern Devon. Sailing up Dodbrook Creek, with the fields of hemp growing lustily on either side and the sun beating down on the muddy stream, you may well wonder whether you are in a tropical river. But nowhere is this impression so strong as in one of the marshy and inaccessible creeks south of Dodbrook where we landed that day. It was a jungle, with trailing creepers festooning the thick trees, and undergrowth so luxuriant that we with difficulty penetrated a dozen yards. Orchids and enormous marsh marigolds glowed in the gloom, and on the many fallen and rotting tree trunks fungi of strange hue seemed to eye us. Even the scents were heavy and exotic, awakening long lost racial memories, as only the sense of smell can.

In the evenings we mostly sat in cafes in Salcombe, which townlet was getting especially interesting as regatta time approached. Here, one would overhear yachtsmen telling of their experiences in homing from France or the North Sea, Cornwall or Cowes, but few completed the story without some reference to the dread bar at the estuary mouth. I myself have lively memories of sailing a Bermuda-rigged racing yacht from Plymouth to Salcombe at regatta time. She was a light-headed boat, built to sail in no wind at all, and to the continuous astonishment of Henry Maxey and myself, who were new to her, she brought us from Plymouth to Salcombe in four hours in what was practically a dead calm. Unfortunately dusk was falling as we reached Bolt Head and the tide was already half an hour turned against us, but we turned the "Flying Dutchman" up the estuary, hoping for another miracle.

Somehow she continued to get wind from nowhere, for it was a dead evening calm, but I shall never forget the alarms of playing blind man's buff in that unlighted estuary, with currents and rocks all over the place and the ship getting wind from quite unknown directions. We made a lucky guess about the bar, but went quite wrong later, for when we were peering into the murk expecting to see lantern pole number three we found the rocks by Fort Charles lunging out of the darkness at us in a most unmannerly way. I flatly denied that the rocks could be in that position, but Maxey, who had long ceased to be surprised at anything in any position, wisely jammed the helm over.

Our acutest discomfort, however, began in the anchorage, which was packed to bursting with yachts of all shapes and sizes, apparently carrying riding lights equally designed to the whims of their owners. The night was clamorous with the noise of engines, of ships' bells, of clinking capstans warping ships round with the tide, and the giant hum of dynamos engaged in transforming yachts into fairy palaces of electric light. Dinghies and picket boats went fussily hither and thither without lights, and consequently, with raucous yells of "Ahoy" and "Blast you, there".

My notion of getting a mooring - a faint enough hope in any case - was to go ashore and ask for one; but Maxey is more experienced in these matters and goes about them with the sublime intuition of the born sailor. He simply raised his voice into the general clamour and demanded of the black night, in all its vagueness, that he be provided with a mooring.

Thrice he bawled, each time adding a few adjectives, and on the last occasion, to my complete astonishment, a hearty and alcoholic voice came from the darkness, telling us to go upstream and await the speaker, who, after taking three more people ashore, would present us with a mooring though he should have to steal it from the biggest yacht in the river!

Scarcely believing this fairy godmother stuff we proceeded upstream and the next moment were flung along the deck by our keel striking something incredibly hard - it was indeed the extension of the ferryman's 'hard' at Salcombe. The calamity was sent by heaven itself, for the next moment a motor boat - or was it a speed boat? - rushed blindly across the space we should have occupied had we gone on. These further evidences of a merciful providence caused us to greet Salcombe Sam (for such he bade us call him) like a long lost brother when, true to his word, he presented us with a mooring five minutes later.

He also gave us, gratis, his opinions on life in general, the most prominent of which, we gathered, was that he "didn't hold with drinking". We thought this a chilling reflection on the warm manner in which we had received him, until he made it clear that he referred to the 'excessive' drunkenness which causes men to fall over the sides of yachts, upsetting the nerves of passing boatmen. We gathered, further, that his objections to drinking were not personal, since he owned to having already that evening sampled the liquor of Kingsbridge, Dartmouth and Salcombe - a most unholy combination.

A searchlight at that moment picked out what was apparently a picket boat full of white-capped and gold-braided naval officers and I innocently asked Sam what warships were here. He gave a guffaw of scorn, "Them baint orficers; them be just bloody little yachtsmen dressed up pretty". With that he warmed to his subject with the fiery eloquence of a revivalist, denouncing the pretentiousness, the hollow mockery of seamanship on every hand, the iniquity, the 'goings on' and above all the drinking. It was, we gathered, not a harbour, but a musical comedy stage.

As if to witness to his words, a pool of limelight played on the lawn of one of the most attractive riverside hotels and into this stepped an Italian singer whose liquid notes soon brought a silence down upon the listening boats and, later, evoked a ring of applause across the water.

Sam endured two songs but at the prospect of having his rugged soul harrowed by yet another of these unsailor-like ditties, his nerve gave way. He rose from his seat and bellowed mixed threats and appeals into the night. From the darkness a loud chorus of "Hear, Hear", echoed by several sailorly gentlemen, shewed that Salcombe Sam was voicing the opinion of an oppressed minority.

Having dealt with this imminent danger, Sam was able to turn his mind in earnest to the drink problem. His eloquence was interrupted by strange pauses which were due (as I discovered when we floated into the light) to Sam gulping from a bottle kept underneath the thwart. The light also revealed the surprising fact that Sam was a relatively young man with crisply curling fair hair and a handsome, intelligent face.

Despite the late hour, the darkness, and the many miles which he had obviously rowed that day, Salcombe Sam cheerfully agreed to row us across to Portlemouth. The men of Portlemouth, he warned us, were savages, and probably cannibals, but even so were infinitely preferable to the sinful visitors of Salcombe, and he, for one, commended our taste in electing to stay the night there. Before he left us we asked him to watch our boat with an eagle eye and to let no one aboard till we should return to sail it in two days' time. This he swore, by bottle and jug, to observe, so help him Neptune. With a parting injunction to beware of drink he rowed back to that sparkling, floating city of sin.

Owing to the weather we changed our plans and decided to take out the yacht next morning. Salcombe Sam was nowhere to be found, and even when we hoisted sail and departed there was no protesting hail from the shore. We could have stolen a dozen yachts. I often wonder if

Sam is still hiding in the lowest pubs of Salcombe from the wrath of those whose boat he imagines he allowed to be stolen.

Now in *Sandpiper* we had spent so long in the creeks and around beloved Salcombe and among the yachts, that we began to feel ourselves loyal members of the colony. For a small-boat sailor, especially after much buffetting by the sea, I can imagine nothing would be more attractive than to stay for ever in these landward waters; but we had a voyage yet to perform, and the sea called - especially after the day on which I had spent several hours stranded on one of the many sandbanks.

So that night at the cottage I spread the chart again and looked at a stretch of dangerous coast between Bolt Head and Bolt Tail, with five-hundred-foot cliffs sloping down to Hope Cove, the grave of a sunken treasure galleon, to greet us at the end. But five pairs of eyes looked over my shoulder at the chart, eager eyes fascinated by the same untravelled coast and ready at once to sign on as crew. Seeing the competition the second mate generously stood back and Joan, who has a low opinion of *Sandpiper,* said that on second thoughts it was all very dangerous. That left Maisie, Jennifer and Virginia, and it was agreed that each should do a section of the trip.

We provisioned and started from Dodbrooke with Maisie as the crew, but the crew was inexperienced and zealously pulled the wrong rope the moment we started so that we crashed against the bridge and buckled a lee board. Our going had been watched with a friendly but critical eye by a sailorly-looking man in the garden of a nearby cottage. Seeing our mishap he threw a rope and hauled us ashore to his garden. Not only did he produce rope and twine and varnish as if from nowhere, but he insisted on our basking on the lawn while he produced tools and repaired the damage with an expertness which left me awed.

This friend in need, whose acquaintance I treasure as one of the choicest gifts which our journey brought us, turned out to be a naval officer who had retired to this cottage to be in close contact with the sea. Twice a day his old friend visited him with gently lapping waves. He would know no more its cruel rages but only the unfailing charm of approach to which it is always lulled by these lake-like, wooded creeks.

In consequence we did not leave till four o'clock in the afternoon, when our old naval friend said good-bye reluctantly - particularly to the three graces - and wished us auspicious winds. But there was no wind then and Maisie and I paddled to Lincombe, the first rendez-vous, which we reached before the reserve crew coming in the car. The planning of combined boat and car expeditions is always amusing; for there is much skill required by those at sea to judge the obstacles likely to be encountered by the land party, and by the latter in estimating how changing winds and currents are like-ly to have affected the progress of those at sea. Again, the spot on the map marked as a rendezvous may prove inaccessible from the land, owing to bad roads, farmers or bulls, or from the sea owing to rocks and reefs. On one such jaunt, both parties arrived at the right cove at the right moment, but the boating party could only wave helplessly up at the land party stand-ing at the top of a completely unscalable three-hundred-foot cliff.

I expected great things when Virginia came aboard,

for she is a born sailor, of a long line of admirals and sea lords. The first was created a baronet when fighting under Nelson and the last was created a peer and lost an arm at Zeebrugge.

Sandpiper seemed conscious of the honour, for she slipped down towards Salcombe with a trim and steady motion as if to say that the Atlantic itself had no fears for her in such competent hands. But presently I became aware that all was not well with the morale of the crew; there was a certain chilly, coldly mutinous spirit abroad. In particular my references to the lovely scenery were not well received. That gave me the clue. By Heavens! yes, it was my ancient braces; for while from the forward seat I could see everything, Virginia had the incomparable view completely wrecked by the blot upon the scenery constituted by my antique trouser gear. For one used to the faultless dress and etiquette of His Majesty's ships it must certainly have been a galling spectacle.

Nevertheless a ship should not be judged by the captain's braces but I refrained from argument for I dislike being cracked on the head with a paddle. Besides it is beneath a captain's dignity to argue with his crew. So Virginia, after a last withering glance at my braces - a glance which shewed she regarded them as a disgrace, a blot on the landscape and a public danger - went ashore at Salcombe. We sadly missed so capable a mariner and so lovely an adornment; indeed, to recall her I would gladly have sunk my cherished old braces in the deepest part of the Atlantic, at whatever danger to the fisheries, but it was too late: for the new crew was already aboard.

This was Jennifer of the auburn curls and that equable temperament which is so valuable in a shipmate called upon to face storms, darkness - and braces. We headed out to sea now with no definite rendezvous at which to meet the land forces. Our intention was to get as far as we could, whilst the land party had to keep us in sight to join us when we landed in a suitable cove beyond Bolt Head. It was evident that we should not get far, for the light was failing.

Past Fort Charles and South Sands we paddled and came to the lofty side of Bolt Head. Massive, eerie and inhospitable it looked in the gathering dusk. On to the next point of cliff, paddling in swinging rhythm, we rode the outgoing tide. Still no sign of sandy cove or of dimpling waters on a tiny beach. Would the cliffs never break: would the land present this stern front for miles and miles? At last a tiny landing place. Jennifer who had been silent awhile, gave a cry of joy and *Sandpiper* leaped again as her round arms sent the paddle deep into the water. It was indeed a landing place, but the cliffs above were quite unscalable!

We turned our backs and paddled seaward again, more desperately. Far above and behind us a light appeared in a cottage. Dimly, astern, Salcombe began to twinkle too, seeming to call us back from the dark sea and the bleak headland.

Surely the coast would give us shelter soon! We were out at the point now, peeping hopefully around the corner. A wide bay greeted us but it was hemmed in with rugged cliffs, bleak and hostile. No beach, no cove, no harbour, no break of any kind. But now it was so dark that we could only make out the shore by the white surge of the gentle swell lifting and falling over the rocks.

From above the high point of Bolt Head came, very faintly, a cry like the hoot of an owl: it was the land party wailing in bereavement; for they had long since given us up for lost. So too had Jennifer, palely silent in the gloom. Evidently we had to go back. We put about and made for the glitter of Salcombe. And that decision prevented our getting to sea for another three weeks; for that same night the spell of fine weather broke and next morning saw the white horses of the south-wester charging to close the gate to the sea.

Chapter 8

Bolt Head to Hope Cove

We were locked in; caught behind an exposed headland by
a fierce south-wester which lashed the sea for a fortnight with a smouldering petulance characteristic of
summer gales. From the security of South Sands we
watched the foam breaking on the Bull and all the rocky
coast as far as Prawle and admitted that, if we were
not to go to sea, there was no 'better 'ole' than
Salcombe estuary in which to be confined.

For we dared the wind, scudding among the little
bays, disturbing the bathers in their revels in the
clear sunlit shallows. Donald Swan - he who had fought
with me the icy rigours of the upper Dart - came down,
complete with the inevitable diary, in which doubtless
all my sins are remembered. *Sandpiper* shewed her
paces in hair-raising cruises among the anchored
yachts, which had become more numerous since the gale
began. In a sudden squall and blinded by a deluge of
rain, we rammed the Salcombe lifeboat full amidships,
removing a yard of paint. Fortunately another rain
squall enabled us to slip away, unnoticed, from imminent 'rescue'.

A south-wester has a spirit all its own, it is for
ever flinging deluges of water down one's back, whilst
wearing throughout an inane grin of bright sunshine. If
you venture to sea in a boat it will begin a foolish
game of hide-and-seek, charging down on you in boister-

ous and destructive glee when you least expect it.

The joke it finally played on us came within an ace of ending our voyage. Donald, the second mate and I were huddled beneath the cliff at South Sands, wearing our overcoats and eating the last of our lunch. Two hundred yards away over the flat sand, *Sandpiper* was pulled up safely in shallow water (like a true wading bird). Down the valley the south-wester flung a squall of wind. I saw *Sandpiper* shudder and begin to move. Without wasting breath on a single word I bounded to my feet and covered the two hundred yards in record time. But *Sandpiper* was then well afloat and bound for the open sea at a great rate. I could wait neither to check my speed nor remove my overcoat: I simply plunged in, wading and swimming until, just as I got out of my depth, my right hand seized *Sandpiper's* departing stern. My left hand, I found, was still clutching a water-soaked Cornish Pasty.

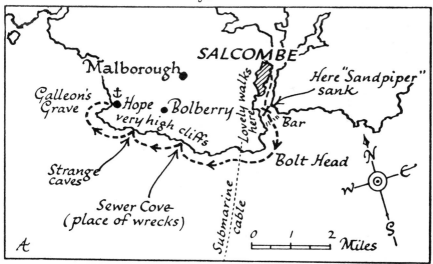

This joke, I am sorry to say, was much appreciated by Jean and Donald, indeed at every recollection of my bolt down the beach they rocked afresh with mirth. But the next joke was on Donald. When the gale was at its worst I donned a bathing costume, put stone ballast in *Sandpiper* and took her out for a supreme test. The waters of the creek were blown almost white and *Sandpiper,* with howling rigging, lay over until the boiling water hissed past her coamings. She dare heel no farther, but it seemed impossible that the wind could blow harder. There was no sign to windward, indeed, the water could register no more distress under the wind; so the south-wester's final blow came unheralded. *Sandpiper* made no fuss; she steadily leant over until her mast-head touched the sea and thus, fighting to the last, she filled with water, and continued on her way under water with the graceful dive of a submarine. That was the only time she capsized under sail.

There had always been a theory that it would be impossible to disengage oneself from *Sandpiper* when she capsized. This I was able to disprove at once; but apparently, from the shore, it looked as if we both had disappeared. Thereat Donald plunged in fully clothed without a second's hesitation. I swallowed pints of water laughing at the spectacle. It was the best bathe I had had for a long time.

Bathing, for that matter, is good in Salcombe estuary, though as in all estuaries, one must appreciate the habits of tidal currents. And at night, with moonlight bathing, it may become dangerous since one cannot quickly observe the direction of drift.

During the two days which elapsed before we got a boat to salvage *Sandpiper* - an easy proceeding for her mast was only a few feet under water at low tide - we went hiking. Upon a bridge linking two points of the garden of one of those lovely villas, set among subtropical vegetation in the Portlemouth valleys, we encountered a notice reading:

"Any person wilfully injuring any part of this County Bridge will be guilty of *Felony* and upon conviction liable to be *Transported* for *Life.*
     By the Court.

SELBY."

Keeping a respectful distance from the bridge we took the first ferry back to Salcombe, seeing new significance in the words which Salcombe Sam had uttered about the Portlemouthians. But perhaps this is the abode of some retired surveyor who has removed from a demolished bridge this reminder of how the colonies were peopled in the good old days.

Now the clear, cool weather and sharp showers, typical of the tail end of a cyclone, gave us notice that the weather had settled again. *Sandpiper* is provisioned, the second mate is called aboard and we put out to sea again under paddles. I wish words could convey how brightly the sun sparkled on the wavelets which frolicked around the great bulk of Bolt Head, as we slipped through the translucent waters over the shallow bar. We paddled strongly for we had to round the headland before the tide should turn upstream. Seaward was a shield of burnished gold and the bright rim of the horizon seemed to promise us a glimpse of fairyland that day.

Nor were we disappointed; for the most glorious scene burst upon our eyes as we rounded the headland. I knew it as a lovely vision from the land but it was doubly glorious from the sea, with all its colours freshly enamelled by the morning sun. Blue water; fantastic cliffs of coral limestone, painted in subtle shades from pink to dove-grey; the vivid emerald of fresh young bracken and all the hues of luxuriant foliage clothing the broad sweep of the valleys.

One knows, as if for the first time, the thrill of the wanderer who comes upon a lovely countryside of hills and virgin woods and realises that no one has ravished it, no treasure has been taken from it, no one subjected it to ownership.

Closer scrutiny of the giant landscape reveals a tiny tumbledown cottage snuggling in the lap of the first coombe, almost at the water's edge. Was it the home of some young fisherman and his lass seeking an idyllic existence in this lone and lovely coombe? Before romance runs away with imagination let me tell you that this little house was built to take in the submarine cable from Brest which was first brought ashore here in 1870. If you poke among the bracken at the top of the low cliff you will find the trenches that were dug in the rock. Under the sleeping ferns of this quiet coombe pass the swift messages which thrill the brain of a nation.

In spite of some protests from the second mate we continue to paddle hard, for we are entering on what is perhaps the most rugged stretch of coast along the whole of South Devon. At times the limestone ramparts are almost bleak and inhospitable, even with the warm sunshine and the friendly sea. There is no real refuge for us until we reach Hope Cove, so despite the friendly smiling ocean, we must get a little nearer to safety before relaxing.

Astern Bolt Head stands out to sea in rugged grandeur, a fitting bulwark to terminate the lofty plateau of the South Hams. Its profile reveals jagged, serrated rocks, like the teeth and tusks of some giant prehistoric monster. Prawle and Bolt Head are the guardians on either side of the gentle estuary, but whereas Prawle sits like a good-tempered lion, Bolt Head is a fierce monster with snarling fangs. All this coast has the air of being borrowed from Cornwall. It is spare and lean and rugged as a hermit. It has the spiritual, other-worldly atmosphere of Cornwall, and something of its bleak monotony; though here it is but an astringent diet between rich feeding on the warm red sandstone scenery of other parts.

Now the pinnacles of Bolt Head sink into toy-like proportions and we find ourselves opposite a little flat biscuit of sand held between jaws of grey rock. It is the only break in all these miles of cliff and is labelled on the map "Sewer Mill Sands", a title which doubtless accounts for it being little visited and one of the few utterly unspoilt coves in Devon. Actually the word 'Sewer' is a corruption of the Anglo-Saxon 'Saewere', meaning the settlement of the sea folk; but I think you will agree with me that this is a fact best not widely known.

Seeing these golden sands in summer one can scarcely imagine how blackly forbidding this coast can be when winter sends the endless, drenching south-wester in blind fury against its battlements.

This is Devon's grim coast of wrecks. One would almost imagine that it stretches a sinister hand out into the Channel to grip passing ships. At any rate such good pilots have come to grief on its stony ramparts that many say the iron in the rocks must at times deflect ships' compasses. It is only a few years since a proud South African liner became a total wreck here. In a cove towards Bolberry, where any sign of human handiwork looks strangely out of place, are the indigestible remnants left by the maw of the sea - an anchor, a huge propeller, boilers and oddments of machinery, half buried in the sand. The years have not subdued its ferocity, for shortly before I wrote these lines, the world's largest windjammer, the *Herzogin Cecilie,* eight times winner of the grain race from Australia, broke her back on the rocks by Sewer Mill Cove. Gallant and forlorn vessel, she was beautiful as a poem even in decay.

Neither have the years subdued the wreckers' spirit of these parts, for the local farmers are said, rightly I believe, to have made a considerable haul by charging thousands of visitors for the right to a near view of the wreck. After this advertisement Sewer Mill will be an unknown cove no longer.

But now the azure heaven continues to smile and we paddle out in a more leisurely fashion, whilst the second mate sings again, by request, "Over the sea to Skye," a song very appropriate to this rocky coast. The cliffs seem to get higher and higher until we lose sight of the green hills altogether.

Ahead, I sight the end of the land - Bolt Tail - and beyond it the faint line of a much lower coast behind the waters of Bigbury Bay. But what is that strange hole in the cliff? It is like the gate of an ancient Egyptian temple and it must be of huge dimensions for it extends to nearly half the height of the cliff. The second mate also evinces great curiosity, so we head *Sandpiper* for the land, scanning the oblong black hole with expectant eyes. Once more, as at Prawle, we glide over an oily sea under the blistering heat of a cloudless sky, but now, all the time, we are conscious of a very gentle swell heaving under the gleaming reptilian skin of the sea.

In a little while we peer up at the enormous blackness of the door in the cliff which even at a dozen yards our eyes cannot penetrate. At the very entrance the water is still fathoms deep and the swell rolls, without pause or stay on into the dark channel of the cave. Perhaps this is the long lost gateway to the underworld! Or the "caverns measureless to man" of which Coleridge wrote in *Kubla Khan*.

The second mate, looking fathoms down at the long tentacles of seaweed waving ominously towards us, begs that we do not go far in, complaining that if *Sandpiper* should upset in that strange darkness she would give one shriek and disappear helplessly. So we glide in very cautiously, keeping our distance carefully between the sheer walls of sweating stone. At once a cold, clammy breath floats towards us, as from some submarine monster resting in the cave. The sharp change from the furnace outside to the icy cool depths of the cave is an extra-ordinary experience.

I don't know how far we went in this manner - perhaps

thirty yards - and then the walls fell back and we found ourselves entering a vast hall. At first we scuttled back to the corridor, for the sensation of losing sight of all solid walls and entering an unspecified region of nebulous darkness was too much for our nerves, but soon we were astonished to see a thin shaft of light falling from somewhere very high up and striking a single pinnacle of rock, which glowed with a pale red light, for we had come upon red sandstone again. Yet it only made the gloom deeper elsewhere: all that we could tell was that we were on quite an extensive inland sea, in which we paddled *Sandpiper* cautiously in circles, tentatively increased in size.

The swell approached with a crescendo of gurgles down the narrow corridor, then spread out into the dark pool, lifting us gently in the darkness and passing on to break some time later on an inland beach. But where that beach was or how extensive, we could neither see nor deduce. We could not even glimpse the white of the breaking wave.

At the thought of capsizing or being shipwrecked on that dark strand, far from the sun and under thousands of tons of rock, I shivered again. Our restless second mate also found the sights and sounds oppressive beyond bearing, for, presently, for the sixth time, she demanded that we get out to the light. We came out into the fierce sun again and found the glare and warmth a heavenly thing; but my curiosity was not satisfied and I planned to come next day with two boats, with torches and ropes.

Unfortunately at Hope Cove there was only one boat to be hired and that was anything but ideal for such an enterprise. Nor was the crew to my satisfaction, for Donald couldn't get down that day and we had to put up with two females who shall be as nameless as they were nautically incompetent. We found two more huge caves, with approaches of the same size and pattern, hidden behind a split-off portion of the cliff, but neither was quite so big as the first and it is probable that we explored their real limits. The great domed pool of the first cave, however, still defied our exploration, for our torches were powerless to penetrate the depths and only succeeded in making darkness darker and the mystery still more mysterious. I placed the Hope Cove boat half-way in from the last light of the entrance and went ahead in *Sandpiper* towards the sounds of the surf on the underground beach, but just as I was getting into shallower water a larger swell than the other

brought the Hope Cove tub down on a rock with a crash that echoed catastrophically through our strange blind world. The females evidently thought some strange monster had taken a kick at the boat and they burst forth into fits of contagious hysterics; so that I considered myself very lucky when I got *Sandpiper,* myself and them out to the open air again.

That evening, in the quiet of Hope Cove, I tried to get the fishermen talking about the caves; but they were strangely reticent and I believe they have a superstitious horror of going near them. For that matter most of the inhabitants of Hope seem to speak generally in monosyllables as if they are saving their breath against some great occasion in the future. Indeed, when I tried to hire a boat that evening all I could get in reply to any question whatever was either 'gone to tea' or 'to-morrow' which became on the fifth repetition 'tea' and 'morrer' - both excellent watchwords for avoiding immediate action, and the avoiding of immediate action seems the ultimate aim of philosophy at Hope.

However, in the "Hope and Anchor", the second mate and I found a native who not only answered questions but emitted whole sentences on his own initiative. It was obvious from the looks of disfavour on the part of the inhabitants that he was regarded in consequence as being completely drunk.

Bolt Tail is one of the very few points in South Devon from which you may see the sun sink into the sea, and that night we watched it throw a red mantle over Hope Cove, and over *Sandpiper* asleep at her moorings above Galleon's Grave.

Chapter 9

Avon, Erme and Yealm

A lotus land where it is always sunny afternoon - that is the picture I shall long remember when thinking of the coast from Hope Cove to the Yealm.

We had left the bleak, iron-grey ramparts behind us and opened up a gentle curving bay of low cliffs, glowing once more with the ruddy welcome of red rocks - the first we had met since leaving Torbay. And with them came lush green fields and wide golden beaches turned ever towards the afternoon sun.

On leaving Hope Cove we were presented by the fisher-men with a fish. To be exact Jean was the recipient, for she seemed to have taken the eye of a certain tall and decidedly handsome red-haired fisher-boy. It was a love token and was a very special kind of fish indeed for I have never seen anything like it before or since, it being shaped like a mackerel but twice as big and coloured like a whiting.

A very helpful, but gutsy and wayward, north-easter ruffled the sea to a deep blue and sped us on our way along by lovely cliffs and coves to Thurlestone. Thurlestone has been for years - and long may it con-tinue to be - a very select settlement of those who golf, fish and like good bathing and no artificial amusements. Everything about it is well done and just a little expensive. The Thurle Stone itself is a rock in the sea with a hole through the centre through which the wind or surf 'thurls' or roars. In stormy weather it is said that its roaring can be heard ten miles away.

Having run in near the Thurle Stone we were forced out to sea again by a line of jagged reefs which must be dangerously hidden at high tide. Though these parts are so respectable now they were once the haunt of the most godless crew of wreckers on the Devon coast.

The story is told of a church service in these parts which was interrupted by someone entering the porch and shouting "A wreck! a wreck!" with the result that the church emptied in two minutes. Some months later, likewise at a Sunday service, the same cry was heard. "Let us pray," said the clergyman, and while his parishioners were on their knees, he made his way quickly to the porch. Arrived there he pronounced "Amen", and added "We'll all start together this time".

Bigbury Island has a finer appearance from the sea than from the village, but we had little time to scan it, for we had to cross the bar at the mouth of the Avon with an inrunning tide and the wind against us.

There is a broad gap to the left of the breaking water and through this we sailed easily and came anon in sight of Bantham. Bantham is a pretty, whitewashed, open village, quite unspoilt, and a resort of small-boat yachtsmen who were even then enjoying their weekly regatta in the swift current and blustering wind.

There seemed to be a likely camping place in the flats by the ferry, but we decided to take advantage of the tide to explore further up the stream. Almost at once the land locked to, with the finality of inter-locking teeth, leaving us as if in some mountain lake. The Avon, like most of these rivers, has its own unique character of beauty. Winding shyly among vaulting hills as high as those of the Dart, it seems cut off from the rest of the world and, indeed, practically no building is to be seen anywhere in its kingdom. It has the charm of utter virgin innocence. Where the stream divides we landed on the central rocky point, with an old limekiln 'castle' and a steep bracken-covered hill behind. From this camping ground it seemed inconceivable that we had ever been to sea: two more hills had crossed their arms between us and the ocean, whilst around were farms and woods and the quiet arms of the lake. Wild birds of the estuary wheeled and called around us.

Here Jean was prevailed upon, with great difficulty, to cook her precious fish for lunch and a very fine dish it made. After which we climbed over the hill to Aveton Gifford. Now all guide books will tell you that the name is pronounced "Awton Gifford", but when I asked a native if I was on the right path for "Awton Gifford" he eyed me suspiciously, and in a manner which indicated that I was a damned fool tampering with ideas beyond my grasp. He replied, "Us calls un Avvytone Jiffurd." So I went to the postmistress, a pretty young woman, who confirmed that it was pronounced as it was spelt. I might thus have gone away with a settled mind had it not occurred to me to ask the local school-master. He reversed these decisions, politely pointing out that as the postmistress had only recently been a pupil at his school and had indeed been taught spelling by him, she couldn't possibly know better than he. With this I finally aligned myself with the school of thought which pronounces the name Awton Gifford. But as I was idling in the street a small boy, who had over-heard my conversation with the headmaster, offered the information that his father and other farmers in the neighbourhood called it "Avvytone Jifford". "'Ee daunt zay wurds prapper," he added, in explanation of his headmaster's default. There will be civil war in Aveton Gifford one day, unless some solution is found.

Next morning the north-east wind was, if anything, stronger, and bore us swiftly with the tide down the curving course of lovely Avon. We shot over the bar at a terrifying speed but, the tide being already low, we dared not cut between Bigbury Island the land. The island is the property of the owner of the hotel, on the landward side, and no other buildings have been allowed to encumber it, so that from the sea-side, it

appears deserted. In the hotel you may see a genuine
old pirate flag nailed to the wall.

Having as much wind as we could stand we thanked
heaven for the lee of the island in which to gybe in
comparative safety. Then we forged ahead over a sparkling sea, enjoying the range of coast from the blazing
white sands of Bantham to the cool green woods glimpsed
at Erme. In the foreground the limestone cliffs are
shot with extraordinary shades of pink and greeny grey
and split in square shiny slabs so that at times one
gets the impression of a tartan plaid draped from the
fields above. All the coast is full of warm colours
which stain the generous wine of sunshine in a thousand
shades.

So swiftly had we sped before the wind that we were
off Erme mouth in an hour and there we decided to land
at a cove called Fernycombe, whence we might climb to a
nearby village, Kingston, to replenish supplies which
were getting very low. How varying are the coastal
farmlands! How one is tempted to make hasty judgments
on the owners! For, having climbed a two-hundred-foot
cliff, we found ourselves faced with devilishly-hidden
barbed wire fences in hedges altogether too decrepit
for Devonshire. An excessive number of cattle walked

moodily about fields bare of all but thistles; indeed, the place was an orgy of barbed wire and thistles. To add to our despair a woman at the farm pointed out two fields with bulls in and added, under the impression that we were trying to get to Fernycombe Cove, that it was quite inaccessible!

I always go to Kingston village when I want to go to the end of all creation, for such it undoubtedly is. All the more surprising, therefore, to find that it has two good inns. Years ago that skilful wanderer of byways, Harper, found Kingston and wrote of it, "There is one inn, the 'Sloop' at which you wait half an hour for tea", but Jean and I were served with lobster mayonnaise, as good as any in Soho, at the "Dolphin" in five minutes, to our eternal astonishment. And I have been to Kingston inns since, in the dead of winter, and found much comfort by their quaint firesides.

From Fernycombe in the afternoon we tacked up the Erme with a fine tide and a stiff wind. The tide played the game well all along the coast, for each morning it brought us down one river and each afternoon it bore us up another.

It is not for me to try truthfully to describe the serene beauty of the Erme, for, as the reader will have gathered, I am irrevocably convinced that it is the loveliest river in Devonshire, and therefore in England. Its mouth, like that that of the Avon and the Dart, hides shyly between lofty hills, but as one enters it smiles at one with fair wide beaches; indeed, the deep cove of Mothecombe would make a playground for a city. In a little while the shadowy woods begin on either side and continue in unbroken perfection as far as one may care to navigate.

The unspoilt nature of this river and of the little villages such as Holbeton which lie inland from it is due to the policy of the Mildmays of Flete, a policy which has its disadvantages if you are compelled to come hither by land, for, as Harper says, "Mothecombe is a place where all explorers are severely discouraged", and hereabouts "the Mildmays have abolished all inns, while their tenants dare harbour no such chancy thing as a stranger".

Soon we went carefully owing to the many sandbanks and the tortuous sweeps of the Channel, which kept us constantly guessing. Never have I seen so many varieties of sea-birds as on these sandbanks; it is a perfect bird sanctuary. There were, of course, the common herring gulls in large numbers and a number of handsome black-headed gulls with bright red legs and beaks. We met an occasional oyster-catcher and, I thought, a few terns, not so easily distinguishable from black-headed gulls except by their swallow-like wings, their wavering flight and their "rick, rick" call.

Dainty little brown-speckled ringed plovers rose in tiny clouds as we approached, uttering a plaintive, musical "toor-lit, toor-lee". There were one or two very long-beaked birds looking like snipe, but most impressive of all were the long scimitar beaks of the curlews, who strutted proudly about the mud banks like very dignified gentlemen in a ballroom. They had doubtless just come down from the moorland breeding haunts for the autumn season by the sea. The wild moors, however, have stamped their souls indelibly, as you will not doubt if you hear their weird, haunting cry, "whour lee", especially when it comes in eerie manner from the darkness, as we heard it many times that night.

Sandpiper scudded about, very much at home among these estuary birds and the mudflats; and well she might have been, for presently we found ourselves among large colonies of sandpipers who seemed to wheel in the air in greeting, flashing their white fronts and thrilling the woodland echoes with their chorus of tremulous, trilling whistles.

At last the stream grew very narrow and we were forced to drop sail and paddle, to avoid striking the arching branches. Here we met birds of a different breed, half a dozen swans and literally hundreds of pheasants who were so tame that they ran along by the boat for us to feed them. We saw many lovely camping spots, but dared not land, for the woods were obviously carefully preserved, so we began looking eagerly for some island or unfenced no-man's-land on which to pitch our tent.

Soon we were delighted by the sight of a smooth-cropped grassy bank, a flat peninsula about three feet above the water. While the second mate went foraging, I pitched the tent. Suddenly I realised that it was a spring tide and that the water, now only a foot from the grass level, was rising.

With what a variety of climate and terrain the voyager has to contend! The previous night we had known the difficulties of house building in Switzerland, trying to secure our tent on a rocky hillside sloping like the roof of a house. This night we found ourselves in a flat and marshy Holland, faced with the problems of drainage and dykes. There was not a moment to lose and I dug like a madman, building a dyke around the little patch occupied by our tent and equipment. Over the lip of the river-bank the waters came, more slowly now, but still rising, and soon the peninsula, which had looked like firm ground, had disappeared in the sea, leaving our small circular dyke-defended island. The dykes being momentarily adequate I dug a hole in the centre of the plot into which all water leaking through the dykes could be drained. In the end the water rose actually to within one inch of the top of the dykes and then gradually subsided, leaving a very damp and miserable world around our small dry island.

To this island Jean presently returned, with tales of the loveliness of Flete Castle - that medieval-looking building erected and matured in the nineteenth century! Half a mile beyond Flete she had struck the main road (whence you may see Flete in all its glory) and had got eggs and milk from Modbury. Modbury is a little and modest old town now, but you may see from its substantial buildings that it was once a very proud capital of this south-western Devonshire; indeed, the elder branch of the Champernownes lived there for generations in great splendour.

As the turbid waters began to pour seaward again the stream became alive with mackerel. I have never seen so many mackerel, in fact, I have never seen mackerel at all so far up a narrow stream. We dipped the paddles in the water trying to scoop them out - the stream was choked with them - but our implements were too crude even for this. With a small net we could have had literally hundreds.

A glorious moon rose over the woods and the night was musical with the varied calls of birds, alike only in their weird, plaintive harmony. Naturally we had some misgivings about the next high tide. I was awakened at six o'clock by the sound of many watery gurglings and a strange thudding and splashing which I could not 'place'. It was caused, I found, by a horse who had taken refuge on our island and who, on my sudden appearance from the tent, bolted precipitately, sending my heart into my mouth, for had his hooves touched the dyke we should instantly have been flooded a foot deep in water. For once I enjoyed a view of the sun rising from his cloudy bed, while the tide, brimming the dykes, peacefully subsided again.

Although the stream is narrow it is deep with the rising tide, and I do not doubt that the Erme could be explored much further by boat, but I was already a little tired of living in Holland so we slipped down the river with the same tide. Tiny Rattisborough Island at the mouth looks big enough to camp upon - not very comfortably, perhaps, but still there is much satisfaction in camping on an island. There appears to be no bar to the Erme and we were soon forging along before the same favourable north-easter, westward to the mouth of the Yealm.

It seemed too good to be true, for the north-easter rarely lasts more than two or three days. And indeed it was too good, for after a calm at midday the south-wester came into its own again and we had to paddle against it like galley slaves. Now the kindly coast of Bigbury Bay with its low cliffs and green pastures, its many inlets and warm, open beaches, comes to an end. Once more the cliffs are high and unbroken, and the stretch from Stoke Point to the mouth of the Yealm loomed forbiddingly before our eyes, for if the south-wester should blow strongly this coast would prove a hopeless barrier between ourselves and the Yealm.

At Stoke Point we landed for a rest and to look at a queer little derelict church on the edge of the cliff, hidden, like the sleeping beauty, in an almost impass- able tangle of trees and brambles. Netton appears to be the nearest village but that is quite a mile away, so the origin of the church and the reason for its present state remain a mystery.

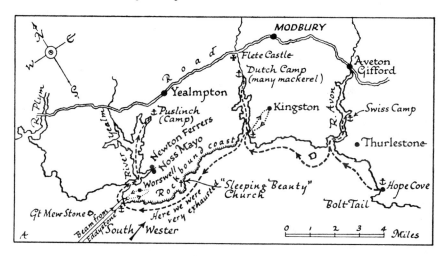

From Stoke we slogged away towards Gara Point in the face of a south-westerly chop. The coast is rocky in the extreme with a peculiar geological formation which allows very narrow gulleys to run far up into the cliffs. They are deep all the way, but with unscalable sides, and no sand at the end - indeed, soft sand is an unknown luxury on this inhospitable coast.

We were weary in the extreme and very wet when at last we sighted a narrow pebble beach. We bent our leaden paddles towards it, not noticing the house and landing stage round a corner of the cliff. As we were about to enjoy the mercy of landing a very fat, dark woman appeared from nowhere and informed us shortly that we could not land as it was a private beach. Then I knew the fury which the Vikings must have felt when, tired of storm and stress at sea, they met a cold

119

reception on shore. Then I realised for the first time that there was full justification for their legendary ferocity. I could cheerfully have fried the woman in her own fat, but I couldn't even express my views in words, for I didn't want the second mate to pick up bad habits.

So we crashed our way into the south-wester again, hopefully looking into every inlet and hopelessly turning away. At five o'clock we reached lovely Gara Point, but we had no eyes for its loveliness, indeed, there seemed nothing to do but scuttle the boat and sink with it, for we had no energy to go further and the wind threatened to sweep us into these most jagged rocks whenever we paused to rest. Then we spotted a most glorious cove, two coves, under the headland! The excitement must have gone to my head for I climbed the cliff and cut heaps of bracken which I dropped in bundles into the cove, to make beds on the pebble beach, although a moment's inspection would have shewn me that the beach was submerged at high tide. The bales had therefore to be hoisted up again, together with all our goods, but the site which we had on soft turf, above, compensated for all our labour.

The coves appeared to be seldom or never visited (which scarcely surprised me) for we found endless supplies of driftwood. For some reason driftwood, in spite of its years of immersion in salt water, will burn very fiercely, giving an intensely hot fire such as is never obtained with ordinary wood. On one cove we found a complete five-course dinner, consisting of grape fruit, dogfish, bird, joint, and a half-emptied demijohn of rum - assembled there by the recent north-easterly breeze and the queer coincidence of tidal currents.

From our new home we caught the first glimpses of the coast of Cornwall - Rame Head - and as the blue of the night spread over land and sea we picked out the flash of the Eddystone far to the south-west.

Towards Plymouth, ships' lights come and go. The moon rises and sinks again, the stars gleam and fade, but the little window of our tent witnesses from dusk to dawn the constant heart-beat of the Eddystone's silvery gleam.

Lovely Gara; a pale green shadow of land making its home in the breezy blue sea: best of both elements, wild and unspoilt yet gentle and inviting. When it welcomed us from our ordeal by exhaustion along that iron coast I had felt like that ancient mariner who greeted the land with "I have come to live and die here". And the morning brought no change of sentiment.

The Yealm was expecting us, but though we were so near we let the day go by. On the hills above we found blackberries bigger than any we had ever seen before and these we combined with cream from Worswell Farm to make food of the gods. What a pleasant contrast in its quiet order and prosperity is Worswell to the farm at which we last landed, and how naturally we were made to feel at home there.

On the following day the south-wester blew quite stiffly. In our sheltered cove we could almost feel the waves thudding on the other side of the thin headland. I have described how watchful of the weather we were at every point of our trip lest we should get stormbound on some open part of the cliff. Storms might rage when we had gained an estuary where we could still enjoy calm water sailing, but we were determined not to be pinned against a rocky coast. Yet here we were in an exposed position and the south-wester was momentarily strengthening.

We could not enter the Yealm till the afternoon for the tide was streaming out until then, but we were so near, only half a mile from shelter, that I swore we would go there whatever the sea. And go we did, though we had to fight our way round Gara Point in a most boisterous sea. Being well rested and near our goal we tackled this violent sea with the utmost zest, giving blow for blow and smashing our way successfully through ferocious blue billows which would certainly have given us a complete sinking feeling at other times. Beyond the Mewstone a cluster of twelve-metre yachts crossing in a smother of foam reminded us that we were approaching Plymouth in regatta time.

The Yealm in its upper reaches is a very beautiful wooded river like the Erme but at the last bend towards the sea, where the Noss Mayo creek runs off, the woods are cut away to make room for bungalows, good and bad, and the yachting colony of Noss. There were many lovely yachts moored here and one of them apparently had on board a troup of chorus girls. Any yachtsman who finds another spending his time moored in a creek immediately suspects him of harbouring chorus girls, or goes about darkly saying "Cherchez la femme". Women and the deep sea are apparently deadly enemies and there are no more adventurous beings than the men who live between the two. To judge by appearances these yachting men had agreed among themselves to say no more about the sea.

Noss Mayo creek is very interesting, if only because of the keen rivalry and separatism between Noss on one side of the creek and Newton on the other, said to be due to the former being a Celtic settlement and the latter Anglo-Saxon. Be that as it may, they are at present similar in being villages with more boatmen to the square yard than you will find anywhere along this coast. Every cottage seems to have its own landing stage, and the boats' painters pass in even through the bedroom windows, presumably being tied to the bedstead or the toe of some sleeping yachtsman.

Out of Noss creek, close hauled to the wind, came a weird rakish-looking sailing boat, with a bowsprit almost as long as itself and a gaff equally gawky. It sailed in a curious mechanical fashion, its scarlet sail spilling the wind awkwardly at intervals. At the last moment, as we gave way to it, I was horrified to see that there was not a soul on board. Thoughts of the tragedy of the *Marie Celeste* passed through my mind: was this to be another unsolved mystery? It went plunging by, but whither I don't know, nor could I stop to do anything about it, for in a strange river with a stiff wind and a frolicsome current I was kept very busy: indeed, at that moment I perforce gybed and shot round the bend.

Except for one or two mouldering stone ruins and a pretty group of houses by the ferry, there is practically nothing to interrupt the soft sweep of the wooded hills which flank the whole of the tidal Yealm and its creeks upstream. It is a scene wholly natural and sweet. One can see above the woods the far grey tors of Dartmoor.

Following the last creek, with a still running tide to help us, we came to the park-like grounds of an old country house - a beautifully proportioned Georgian house, modified in style by a mansard roof - a house looking as if it had once known rich and liberal times but now with half its rooms closed down. An old man with fishing gear, who was mooring his boat as we arrived, proved to be the owner. Not only did he give us permission, in a most gracious old-world fashion, to make use of his grounds, but he walked down half an hour later to point out that at the place we had chosen to camp we should be flooded by the spring tide. It seemed incredible, for we were on a high grassy bank among trees, but that night the water came to within an inch of the mark he had made for us on a tree and to within two inches of the floor of our tent. And in the chilly dawn I saw swans swimming where the peak of our tent would have been.

Chapter 10

To Plymouth and the Tamar

A river, especially one sunken between hills, is a stretch of water designed to bring madness upon any yachtsman used to the honest breezes of the sea. For, whatever the real direction of the wind, the funnel of the river diverts it into blowing either directly up or directly down the stream. And by the well-known law of natural cussedness it is down when you want to go up and up when you want to go down.

I had been astonished, therefore, when the wind had taken us right up the river on the previous night, but I was downright incredulous when I found a north-easterly breeze waiting to take us down the river next morning. Indeed, if that wind held we should be taken to Plymouth and beyond in record time. So we crept aboard quickly and quietly, hoping the wind wouldn't notice us, and shot forthwith past the woods of Yealm at an exhilarating speed, wind and tide being together.

But what was this strange, red-sailed, gawky vessel sailing out of Noss Mayo Creek? It was the *'Marie Celeste'* of the previous evening, and, as I saw with unbelieving eyes, there was again no one on board! She went on like a sleepwalker, mysteriously missing moored yachts and other obstacles. As it was still very early there was no one to salvage her this time, so we came up to the wind and boarded her.

There were some boys on the beach, who looked as if

they would like a boat to play with. They were delighted with the present, but a little puzzled by our instructions to find a man who looked like a lunatic and give him back his boat.

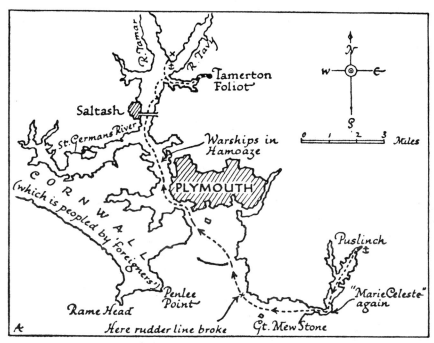

As we turned westward to Plymouth from Yealm Mouth a graceful pyramid of an island stood full in our course, a little more than half a mile out to sea. This is the famed Mewstone, landmark for all who enter Plymouth Sound. It looked the biggest island we had met, but as it is only four acres, that title must really go to Borough Island at Bigbury.

On the gentler slopes of the eastward side we sighted a small cottage, possibly the home of Samuel Wakenham and his wife, the Lord and Lady of the Isle way back in 1830, and the last residents on its shores. Recently the whole island was sold for £500 and given to the daughter of Lord Chelmsford as a wedding present. It would certainly appeal to honeymoon couples.

Although there is a landing spot on the north-west

corner we held on to our course, while the wind was good, the second mate registering the usual protests at this procedure. There is a necklace of rocks between the island and the shore, of which deeper-keeled boats should beware.

We rejoice in typical north-easterly weather. There is a greyness in the sea and a short steep pattern in the waves, whilst the scenery is hard and clear. Every wind has its characteristic and unmistakable command of the mood of land and sea. With the south-wester the horizon turns hazy, and the world becomes bigger and more vague. A greenish sea beats on a land of lustrous colour, sleepy with warmth. When the south-wester bursts into fury the waves come in endless irregular masses, like a horde of mounted barbarians thrust on relentlessly by some pressure behind. Each wave is a character in itself, incalculable, fearless, but tired - a weary giant who will wreck you in his sprawling carelessness, without malevolence.

Across the ago-old battlefield of crafty north-easter and bold south-wester the dread easterly gale, lord of war, sends at rare intervals his sounding chariots and invincible battering rams. His enormous white steeds and iron faced warriors carry everything before them.

In those, unfortunately, still rarer, occasions when these fierce winds cease to contend, the lovely south wind may steal gracefully across the deserted waters. At the first breath of her approach the sea puts on a mantle of the softest azure and becomes spangled with flashing gems of gold and silver. The land bathes in a light which may only be called celestial, whilst sleek wavelets, soft-breasted as doves, make a laughing procession towards the shore.

To run before the south wind is to know the serenity of a floating cloud. The only sound intruding on the silence that stretches far over the hazy horizon is the musical chatter of wave to wave, the rippling laughter and the far-spreading sighing as wave slips into the embrace of wave.

A sharp unceremonious tug at the sail reminds me that to-day we are under the sway of that martinet the north-easter. His orderly rows of hard steely waves march with cold-blooded ferocity towards the west, on into the kingdom of their mortal enemy the south-wester. Every now and then one falls with the cold, silvery flash of a fish's belly. The scenery hardens and the outline of the cliff is sharp and somehow ominous.

Penlee Point stands out clearly ahead as we pass the Shag Stone with its miniature lighthouse (which has no light). Now we have to decide quickly how to cross Plymouth Sound. The wind has veered a little towards east - excellent in direction but now excessive in strength - and in a small boat we must always beware of running too far before a fair wind which, over many miles of sea, may raise such a swell as to sink the boat it has brought so far. A timely reminder of such dangers occurred at that moment for, with a sudden yawing of the boat, one of the rudder lines broke. By the greatest good luck it was the port line and by pulling the starboard line I was able to sail not too clumsily towards the nearest land - Rennie's Rocks - where some very Heath Robinson repairs were effected with string and a bit of rusty wire.

This was but the beginning of trouble, for when we put out again we found much water rising in the boat. Jean was put to baling but was so fascinated by the view now breaking on us that she put as much water back into the boat as she lifted out.

Ahead was the breakwater and the woods of Mount Edgecumbe - that glorious Mount Edgecumbe which "So affected the Duke of Medina Sidonia that he resolved it for his own possession in the partaging of the kingdom", after the Armada should have done its work. Then came the three-mile stretch of white limestone bays, of green parks, battlements and spires constituting the incomparable panorama which Plymouth presents to the sea. To the left, up the Hamoaze, we glimpsed the sombre grey fighting tops of battleships. A cluster of masts of fishing boats filled the old harbour in the centre, and to the right floated a squadron of graceful flying boats, guarded by the vigilant fortress of Mount

Batten.

Other towns of Devon may call to dream or to sleep, but Plymouth is a city in which to live and work. It is much alive where some other grand old towns of Devon are dead. Resounding with echoes of a great past - of Drake, the Pilgrim Fathers and its long association with the Navy - it yet lives in a ferment of ideas of to-day, retaining a capacity to act, preserving and creating its own beauty. Its very slums are picturesque, washed with sunlight and a breeze from the sea.

The Tamar and the Plym, twin moats to the city, prevented its sprawling across the scenery in the days before city councils thought of preserving scenery, and forced it to make of the Hoe and the adjacent parts a civic centre fitting to that noble situation. The Hoe is to Plymouth what Princes Street is to Edinburgh or the Rialto to Venice and is undoubtedly the finest promenade in England, with its endlessly varying view of the Sound, Drake's Island, the Breakwater and Mount Edgecumbe. Its further glory is that it is practically unchanged since, in days long gone by, people gathered upon it to watch the departure of expeditions of war and exploration, wishing godspeed to beloved comrades, first with singing, then with music and, finally, as the ships faded towards the horizon, with a last thunder roll of cannon.

I often think that Plymouth Sound is constructed for an immense natural theatre adapted to some stupendous spectacle. The terraced Hoe provides the stalls and gallery; Mounts Batten and Edgecumbe the royal boxes, and at night the winking of lights of a host of buoys in the fairway make footlights to the curtain of the breakwater.

But across that vast stage at the moment of which I speak there crawls nothing more insignificant than the tiny wind-blown speck which is *Sandpiper*. At first, frightened by the high wind and the water rising in the hold, we had thought ingeniously to cross the rough expanse of the Sound by clinging as it were behind the handrail of the breakwater and then making a short dash to the Hamoaze, but a lull in the wind gave us courage and we ventured straight across.

We had been so engrossed with the spectacle of Plymouth that, until they were almost upon us, we failed to see two big liners steaming to anchor inside the breakwater. One was English, the other German, fluttering the Nazi flags. She looked like the *Bremen,* but when we sailed under her bows we perceived the name *Caribia.*

How many visitors from all corners of the earth must get their first impression of England and the English at Plymouth! Sometimes sophisticated ambassadors; sometimes simple savages, like Pocahontas, who came in here on June 3rd, 1616, accompanied by the faithful Tomocomo, still determined to cut a notch in his staff for every white man he saw, and now reduced to bewilderment by the crowds on Plymouth Hoe. What, I wondered, were the thoughts of these homing Germans in the *Caribia* as they gazed on this Queen of Harbours, this jewelled strongbox of English sea power, this fountain of English colonising enterprise?

Gently now, for the wind is slack, we sail to seaward

of Drake's Island, mysterious pocket fortress with steel eyelids shut tight over its many apertures. There are many strange obstacles, buoys and concrete shapes in this narrow entrance to the Hamoaze - teeth in the lion's jaws. On one of them sit three big black cormorants looking so mysterious and wise that if I were one of the Lords of the Admiralty I should consult them as oracles regarding our future on the sea.

Favourable wind and tide brought us from the secluded woods of Yealm to this great city; we hoped the same wind and flood tide would suffice in the afternoon and evening to take us far up the Tamar to some equally secluded roost.

Entering the Hamoaze I am reminded of the first time I sailed among the fleet there, in 1913, and of my boyish delight in recognising all the great battleships. There were fussy picket boats, carrying handsome, stern-faced officers and crowds of blue-jackets, full of infinite resource and high spirits. Above all I loved the shining, intriguing technical gadgets, products of the mind of man forced to closest grips with reality. That evening there had been a blood-red sunset over Cornwall and we became strangely silent as the great silhouettes passed by; ship after ship, solemn, majestic, impregnable.

Was there some premonition in the half-sad silence that descended on our boyish noisiness? I doubt it; but there certainly must have been brains in those black iron citadels facing at that moment the imminence of a death struggle in which we might lose for ever our ancient supremacy. Within six months three of those ships, including one we had visited, were at the bottom of the sea, with most of their faithful crews.

Once more we sail between anchored dreadnoughts, now gaily decorated with bunting, for, as we soon discover, it is Plymouth Navy Week. The ships' bands are playing spiritedly. On one ship people are dancing to a waltz by Strauss. How colourfully the splashes of summer dresses stand out against the staid, soft blue-grey of the battleship's hull, and how the brass and copper work twinkles in the sun. This is the Silent Service shewing what it can do when it makes a bit of noise.

We slip on past a destroyer, the hull of which is jet black, as if in mourning, and proceed on past a vast aircraft-carrier, shaping our course towards the scattered grey houses of Saltash. Now comes an aircraft-carrier, a momentous structure, something that was not there when we sailed here on that red July evening twenty years ago. What will be on these waters twenty years hence, if we are spared to sail here again, and will another war have converted to scrap iron the magnificent engines of war which float so proudly around us now?

Now we leave the sound of the bands and float on past the docks at Keyham where the smiths of the Navy do their real work of construction and repair. There are destroyers on the slipways and there are huge battleships in hospital, wearing dressing gowns of pale sky-blue with great scarlet bandages of red lead upon their hulls; how all their dignity vanishes in this piebald costume! They have now no more dignity than a gasworks or Brighton pier on bank holiday. And farther down we came upon the sadder but more dignified spectacle of old ships being broken up; ships that have seen service in all parts of the world; ships that have been a home for many a jolly ship's company; ships that have been scorched in the fire of war, and now lie in these creeks derelict, rust-begrimed, dismantled. We felt we wanted to go over and speak to them in their loneliness and desolation. For me there is nothing quite so melancholy as an old ship falling to pieces in some deserted creek. One thinks of the crews who have loved the ship's movements, of the great tempests from which she has successfully sheltered them. Probably they too are dead and gone now, else surely they would come back to rescue their companion from this oblivion.

My thoughts were not permitted to dwell long on this desolate scene on our starboard beam, for my attention was swung in the opposite direction by a rapturous cry from Jean, who points out to the westward a magnificent stretch of wild and wooded creek.

It is the St German's or Lynher River on the Cornwall

side, which goes on up to Polbathic and Landrake and rises in the hills near Pensilva. It looked glorious in the afternoon sun; indeed, had it not been in the foreign land of Cornwall I should have been tempted to assert, in my momentary enthusiasm, that it was the loveliest thing I had yet seen. Verily, it is well worthy of exploration. We resisted the temptation, saying, "on the way back", which, in the end, of course, meant "not at all."

At this point, turning towards the great span of Saltash Bridge, epic achievement of that original engineer Brunel, we were alarmed to see in front of us a

terrifying array of red flags on barges anchored off the Admiralty Pier. These proved to be supplies of high explosive for the fleet. The discovery, I confess, caused us to deflect our course very little, for we felt that in our tiny boat we should be blown to smithereens with equal thoroughness whether we were a yard or a quarter of a mile away, so we satisfied our curiosity and sailed as near as a vigilant sentry would allow. On the hills to the left we saw innumerable well protected gasometer-like constructions, probably reservoirs of oil fuel for the fleet; how precious this store of oil would become in a war which resulted in our being blockaded!

Saltash is a grey tumble-down place, a very poor relative of Plymouth and, in Brunel's high curved bridge, Plymouth seems to shake hands with it in cold and distant politeness. As we passed under the bridge the scenery, which had hitherto been definitely of the sea, noisy with ships, lined with docks, tidal and salty, changed with dramatic suddenness into pleasant, soft, rural seclusion. One floats on a broad river between low green hills and farmlands. Here too the wind left us suddenly as if its commission ended abruptly with the boundaries of the sea. Noisy steamers, upon which hitherto we had gazed with disdain, now succeeded in awakening our envy. A paddle steamer, coloured like a bird of paradise, in a combination of green, cream, pink and blue, went on up the river ahead of us and soon disappeared into some recess of the rather toy-like, sunlit countryside, framed between the austere pillars of the bridge.

It was a lovely mellow evening now and we thought it time to camp while the light was still good. Landing not far from Tamerton Foliot we proceeded to erect a tent in a promising-looking field. It was not until the last pegs were driven in that we discovered we had an interested companion in the form of a large South Devon bull; if you know the size of a South Devon bull you will wonder how we had managed not to see him earlier! I took an immediate dislike to this creature and his inconsiderate arrival, but he, on the other hand, shewed every sign of being greatly attached to us and even put an exploratory head inside the tent. Needless to say we got the things back into the boat in record time, but as there was a good landing place only fifty yards further on, separated from this field by a stout hedge, we were not long in erecting the tent again. Imagine our surprise therefore on looking up from our work to discover another bull - no, it was our old friend himself - standing by like an unemployed person watching street repairs; that hedge was a delusion!

This time we put to sea again in high dudgeon and were almost persuaded to commit the disloyalty of going on to the Cornish side. However, in a little while, we came to the point where Tavy flows into Tamar, and on the point of land between them we found an excellent camping spot.

We had covered seventeen miles that day, a record run, yet done with extreme ease; an object lesson in the proper use of wind and tide but, alas, not one which we learnt straight away. It takes sixty years to achieve the old sailor's true proficiency with the wind and tide. And we had not finished yet, for the evening was still young and we had a great desire to explore the creek to Tamerton Foliot, which beckoned, with an air of mystery, under the viaduct opposite to us. A light evening breeze carried us down this little, forgotten stream; it is incredible that a place so utterly unspoilt, nay, so wild and remote, could yet be geographically near to Plymouth. We sailed on very peacefully past the wooded countryside and occasionally passed very old and deserted-looking cottages, shaping our course all the while towards Tamerton. Here again we met, as we had met so surprisingly in several other remote creeks, a party of singing children coming down through the woods to meet the tide and bathe. Their merry shouts and the sounds of splashing followed us up the river.

Tamerton Foliot is an unspoilt little place, unconscious of itself, and offering nothing to the visitor who wants to be treated as a visitor. A crowd of cheeky children crowded around us at the jetty and when I came back with a loaf I found that Jean had already made friends and knew the names of most of them. Indeed, she had invited two aboard, at which privilege they were duly awed and impressed.

As we sat later by our camp fire in the twilight, singing boat loads came down the river, homing to Plymouth. Plymouth must be a most agreeable city to live in when one can have such beautiful trips on any evening. The intervals between the boats became longer and longer: it was very, very still. In the woods above Cargreen (what an Irish-sounding name!) a woman's voice was singing very beautifully to the strumming of a ukulele; then all was quiet. Below Cargreen I could dimly discern the outlines of the hill above Landulph.

I stand staring into the darkness, seeing ghosts, when suddenly the perfect silence is broken by the chatter and gurgle of a little wave breaking along the pebbles at my feet. It is the bow wave of the boat that I heard passing downstream perhaps ten minutes ago. During the intervening time that little wave has been speeding alone and silent through the dark - a message from them to me. So the waves of our actions pass down the centuries to break at the feet of people yet unborn.

Chapter 11

Tavistock and

Tavy Country

The night, which had settled down with such disarming quietness and sleepy warmth, ended with a crash of thunder which brought me to the tent door wondering whether the powder barges at Saltash had blown up.

Torrential rain flooded our carelessly stowed gear, and the lake-like face of the estuary was whipped into grey, foaming waves, hungry as those of the open sea.

To the north-east, over the lofty grey peaks of King's Tor, Peak Hill and Sheep's Tor, curious, curling columns of smoky cloud stretched towards us like giant's fingers or the tentacles of some gigantic monster penned within the fortress of the moors. It was an astonishing sight, yet not so astonishing as the cataract of water which presently descended from them.

"It can't rain like this for more than five minutes," I said, repeating like a novice the fallacy of all strangers to the moorland rains. In half an hour the torrent had only redoubled itself. Presently, like Noah, I began to take a professional interest in it. Stretching out a hand from our one-piece rubber tent, I recovered a glass jar, empty the previous night and now having exactly an inch of rain in it. In three-quarters of an hour we had as much rain as London gets in a month! Then with miraculous suddenness the morning sun flooded everything - the cloudburst was over. That is how Devon succeeds in holding at the same time the

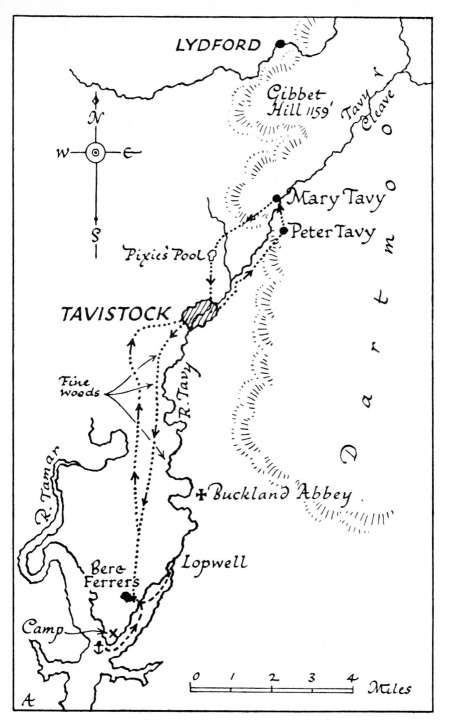

LYDFORD

Gibbet
Hill 1159'

Tavy Cleave

N

W · E

S

Mary Tavy

Peter Tavy

Pixie's Pool

TAVISTOCK

D a r t m o o r

Fine
woods

R. Tavy

R. Tamar

✝ Buckland Abbey

Lopwell

Bere
Ferrers

Camp ✕ ⚓

0   1   2   3   4   Miles

A

sunshine record and the rainfall record. The simultaneous possession of those two records is half the secret of the vigour and abundance of all green things in this fair country.

To-day we would explore the Tavy up to Tavistock. True, the tide was all wrong, but we had been slaves of the tide long enough. Our unusually vigorous paddling unfortunately proved too much for *Sandpiper*. She wept with a bad leak very soon and we had to find our way through gleaming mud banks, by a row of crazy posts in the river, to Bere Ferrers, a quiet, grey little river village, so beautifully situated that it might have been created as part and parcel of the woods and the river themselves.

The son of the house at the post office gave us his last cycle patch with which to repair *Sandpiper* - no mean sacrifice in so outlandish a place - but our warm feelings for Bere Ferrers were somewhat shaken by the imprecations and incantations of an old witch at the staithe. When I said "I beg your pardon", she fixed me with the Evil Eye and announced that Tavy stream had drowned one soul every year, adding mincingly that this year she was rather late. She then settled down to watch our departure with an air of agreeable expectancy which fairly gave us what I believe is technically known as "a fit of the Willy's".

The stream was very swift and as we approached the deep woods and waving reed banks of Lopwell it brought us to a standstill, in spite of furious paddling. Something was wrong with our calculations, for the tide should now have been at the calm of the ebb. I have described how, in the Exe, the tide turns some hours later far up the river than at the mouth; but this was more than lateness.

At first I ascribed everything to the witch at Bere Ferrers, but on reading the newspaper next day I decided the uncanny circumstances were due to the cloudburst which had sent wheelbarrows floating down Tavistock streets that morning. At any rate we were beaten and had to cling to overhanging branches to save ourselves from being swept away. Some day I will tackle

Tavy stream on the fullness of a spring tide and sail into Tavistock itself; for natives of great judgment tell me that these deep, meandering and wooded gorges constitute the grandest scenery south of the moors.

No man who visits the West Country should permit himself to be baulked of viewing sturdy, granite Tavistock, embowered in her woods and preserving still the spirit of her sons - Drake, William Browne, mellowest of Elizabethan poets, Captain Rich-Peake and many other individuals of strong personality and reckless courage.

Tavistock has the reputation among Devonians of being a kind of wild, untamable Far West, where men are men and life insurance is high. Still, to-day, one of its chief exports consists of he-men for the less civilised parts of the Empire. One of these, who was a great friend of mine, having given me a black eye when we were both small boys, found the sheriffs of America too interfering and Mexico too civilised. The wilder parts of Australia staved off boredom for a time, but in the end he was compelled to come back to Tavistock to be in the company he loved. His lightning lassoo is the wonder of all who have to round up moorland cattle and his capacity for liquor is a subject of sermons.

Briton, Roman, Irishman, Saxon and Dane have fought over the jewel that is Tavistock, and it is not surprising if the survivors are a little tough. In 997, thirty years after Buckland Abbey had been built (it lies on the hillside to our right), the Danes took Tavistock, burnt the Minster, and retired with much booty, to the great chagrin of the reigning monarch, Ethelred the Unready. Next came Irishmen from Kerry, as witness those runic stones in the present vicarage garden. One of these saints built an abbey which has lately been rather shamelessly pulled down to to make way for a pub.

For my part I like Tavistock men, whether they shoot sheriffs or linger over love lyrics, but it cannot be denied that, as one good Devonian has said, 'There was and is an ancient prejudice against men of Tavistock. In Tavistock it is ascribed to jealousy. Outside Tavistock they do not attempt to explain, but act upon it, with the promptness of three Okehampton men who, seeing a pedlar struggling in a flooded brook which was washing him away, were about to help him out, when one said: "Augh, tes aunly a Tavistock man, let'n goo!" Which they accordingly did without remorse.'

Not that Okehampton men can be considered much better; indeed, all this western corner of Devon, from Okehampton to Tavistock, hiding from the rest of Devon behind the desolation of Dartmoor and deeply cut up by river cleaves, is a wild region, aptly peopled by a wilder breed than the rest of Devon knows. Its true capital is Lydford, not Tavistock, and Lydford is, or

rather was - for it is nothing at all now - a refuge of lawlessness and devilry even exceeding anything in Tavistock.

In Lydford Gorge ruled the rugged tin miners of Dartmoor. They formed a community which was so powerful as to be beyond the law - and which consequently soon formed its own laws. Its story constitutes a very lively page of Devon history, and leaves echoes in many moorland customs, legends and rhymes, such as the following:

Hast ever heard of Lydford Law
How in the morn they hang and draw
And sit in judgment after?

If you doubt the sinister character of this region; if you scoff at its strange legends of vampires and witches, pixies, ghoulies and ghosts, and of the Devil squealing before St Michael at Brentor; then leave your boat, as we did, and wander through the woods, coming through the dusk by Peter Tavy and Mary Tavy, by Lydford Gorge and canon-like Tavy Cleave and so down the "Valley of Waterfalls" until you see the Pixie Pools (the real Pixie Pools of Devon, these) beneath the moonlight. Then you will know that the eerie spell under which we went our whispering way was not pure superstition and woolly-headedness, begotten of too much cider and a touch of rheumatism.

Chapter 12

To Morwellham?

The Rain Gods of Dartmoor must have been angered by our attempts to penetrate their fastnesses through Tavy Cleave, for at midnight they flung down that drenching, persistent West Country rain which makes one think the atmosphere has turned liquid for evermore.

Tavistock has an ancient reputation for rain. It is recorded that Charles I who once stayed there, had his little joke about it. If anyone remarked that the day was exceptionally fine he would reply, "But it is undoubtedly raining at Tavistock." Charles never loved Tavistock, for, in spite of its inhabitants' passion for fighting abroad, there was a complete lack of enthusiasm for the Civil War. The citizens talked about "removing the war to other parts" and committed the solecism of arranging a local peace between Cavaliers and Roundheads.

By what was supposed to be high noon of the next day (one loses count of time under these unchanging, leaden skies) we had nothing but a tomato and a bottle of sour milk standing between us and starvation. Having no dove to send out over the waters we decided to trek inland and see what we could find. The piece of land where we camped is practically an island between the Tamar and the Tavy and no road crosses to it until one goes about six miles up the Tavy or ten miles up the Tamar. This large diamond-shaped peninsula is curiously different

from both Devon and Cornwall. It is a little princi-
pality of its own, unnoticed and consequently missed by
the march of time. For a mile and a half we climbed
slowly, meeting no roads whatever, and then we suddenly
came on a very old-fashioned farm house. We knocked
somewhat timidly at the door, feeling that the appearance of a stranger must cause some consternation in
such a place. A charming young woman, quiet as a mouse
and pretty as a fairy, invited us in; I had a weird
feeling that it was all out of a fairy story and that
presently a witch would appear and change us into
water-rats (which we should not greatly have minded,)
or, more likely some fierce old ogre. Sure enough, with
a slow, crashing step on the stairs, a real ogre appeared - a dark, hairy man of tremendous girth, who
looked as little like a Devonshire farmer as anyone
possibly could. He might have been a Greek, a descen-
dant of Ulysses from the wanderings of that worthy
beyond the Pillars of Hercules.

There was a strange air of old-world cunning about
him. One felt that he was an atavism, a member of some
ancient race of men which had lived on unnoticed in
this lost, isolated world. He drank us in for a long
time without speaking, wearing the sort of anticipatory
leer that the giant must have bestowed on Jack; he
summed us up shrewdly as strangers to the land, and
sold us eggs and other things at nearly double the
market price. The little mouse seemed acutely conscious
of this knavery but went about quietly and fearfully
under his hypnotic eye. Upon my volunteering that we
were camping on the spit of land between Tamar and Tavy
he announced affably, and with an admirable lack of
hesitation, that he would only charge us 3s. a night
for this privilege. Perceiving, as I paid this, that he
was making a shrewd estimate of how much my purse still
held, I decided that it was time to be going; I also
decided, from a glance at his bulk, that he was unlike-
ly to walk to the river to see just how many nights we
might stay, so we cautiously paid for one night only.

Leaving this old brigand, we penetrated further inland to see what the capital of this little country

would be like. Bere Alston stands right at the centre of the peninsula, on the rounded apex of the pyramid. It is the only town therein, with the exception of its port, Bere Ferrers. We found a fairly large collection of grey and white-washed houses, sleeping in the warm afternoon sun and looking as if nothing had happened to them for hundreds of years. Bere Alston is a farmers' town, knowing no visitors, bereft alike of any signs of modernity or of self-conscious, sophisticated age. We liked it very much and it took us to its bosom unobtrusively and as a matter of course.

Next day, seizing the flood tide early, we started off for our final journey up the Tamar. Cargreen, with its little houses clustering around the "Royal Oak" at the water's edge, and its little street winding up to the church on the hill, looked very inviting, but, sighting the grand scenery before us, we went swiftly on in the morning sunlight.

At Hole's Hole (was it wholly Hole's?) the cliffs began; at least they looked like cliffs, but somehow the people of the neighbourhood have managed to make gardens grow upon their vertical sides. At several points higher up the Tamar we came across this extraordinary cultivation of surfaces apparently sloping almost perpendicularly and on which the gardeners must have had to work roped like Alpine climbers. These gardens are extremely fertile I am told, having the southern sun vertically upon them and catching abundant rain but letting it drain off quickly.

The gentle undulating scenery that had held since Saltash now disappeared; high hills closed in upon the river. Tamar has the charm of most South Devon rivers; it is a 'ria', a river which in its remote childhood has played or meandered on like a river of the plains, in sinuous loops, after which the land has lifted itself, forcing the river now to chisel its easy meanderings in hard stone through deep gorges and valleys. Now we came to Pentillie Castle, looking like a castle of the Rhine, half hidden in the steep wooded slopes of Mount Ararat. Pentillie Castle has the reputation of being the loveliest seat in the West Country, and I can well believe that it is. There seemed to be no villages and the only place we passed in the next two hours was a tiny cluster of cottages at Halton Quay.

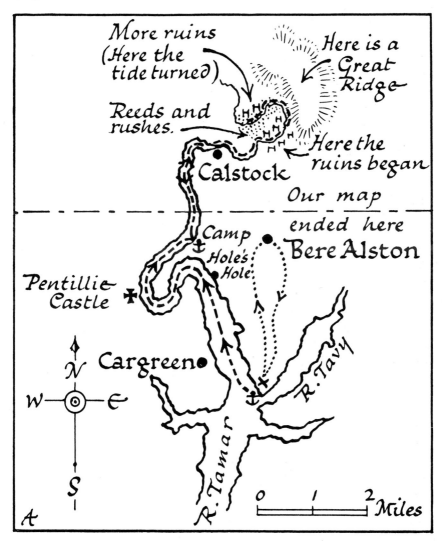

What little wind had helped us on the first stretch of river now dissolved completely. Ever since the north-easterly weather had set in at Hope Cove we had been losing with delicious ease the habit of hard paddling. We were fast approaching the true fisherman's philosophy that unless a place can be reached by wind or tide, it is, to all right-thinking people, inaccessible. No true member of this free-masonry will lower his dignity by rowing or paddling more than twenty yards. So at midday, with the tide about to ebb again, we put in at the back of a hill, the other side of which, owing to the twists of the river we had passed four miles down.

Entering the creek we came upon the astonishing sight of a long whaler, like a Viking boat, evidently preparing to put to sea. A troop of sea scouts swarmed hither and thither, clearing away all traces of their camp. Part of this clearance consisted in heaving firewood into the river - a proceeding which was arrested by a yell of anguish from myself, for dry firewood had been worth its weight in gold to us during the rains. An amicable settlement was reached, indeed, quite a lot of barter occurred between the camp-breakers and the camp-makers, according to the best principle of economics: "small profits and quick returns." Their captain told us they had camped for twenty-five consecutive summers in that creek, and he bade us guard it well.

The big cooking pot bubbled in the centre of the boat, the bronzed faces laughed farewell and the oars came up in salute as these friends of an hour gave us good-bye. Just so, and with such a threshing of oars on the outgoing tide, the colourful Viking ships faded down this river long ago.

The fresh and sunny evening, and the swift inrush of the tide, beginning about seven o'clock, were responsible for setting our minds on the perfectly mad intention of sailing up the river the same evening, and returning to our camp with the ebb tide. Our calculations that the tide would turn about ten o'clock and bring us back by one, ignored all we have ever learnt about tides. We forgot that there was no moon at all, and recked nothing of the fact that the region was entirely strange to us and that our tattered map cut

146

short its story completely at Bohetherick, only a mile upstream.

As we started on this ill-fated expedition the hills, which previously had lunged at the river from either side, across stretches of rush and meadows, closed in to squeeze the stream in a rocky channel between steep slopes, wooded to the water's edge.

Through this lovely but rather shadowy and eerie canon we made good progress on a swift tide, seeing nothing but very occasional thatched cottages, until, round a sudden bend in the rocky channel, we came in view of a lofty viaduct and recognised the massed grey houses of Calstock, fighting their way up the steep hill from its quayside.

So far we had merely reached the limit of navigation by river steamers. Calstock, in the sixties and seventies of the last century, woke to life as the centre of a mining rush, copper and more precious metals having been discovered in these great hills. An old inhabitant told me he could remember well the roaring seventies, when people in Calstock slept six in a bed and the inns sprang up like mushrooms. To-day, Calstock has a distinctly widowed look, but the tradition of mining has stuck and her sons have gone out to South Africa, California and Klondyke. I met in Paignton one old copper-coloured Calstockian directing a fleet of motor boats which were the fruits of gold mining in Africa.

I have described the eerie gloom of the gorges below Calstock. Particularly I remember the very beautiful thatched cottages below shadowy Cothele Creek, darkly crouching in the hollows of the wood, seeming to watch us with brooding, melancholy windows. There too a little chapel peeps out of the woods. It was built as a thanksgiving by Sir Richard Edgecumbe; for at this spot, when pursued through the woods by the king's soldiers, he was minded to throw a boulder into the water and leave his cap floating on the surface, a ruse which sent the soldiers back with the tale that he was drowned. A more gruesome story occurs in the Edgecumbe annals, concerning that Lady Edgecumbe who died early in the nineteenth century. She had been buried some hours in the family vault when the villainous sexton returned to steal her jewels. As he tugged at the ring on her finger she rose upright in the coffin. No one sailing through these woods in the gathering dusk, as we did, could doubt that even more eerie things might happen at any moment.

Calstock had come as a distinct relief and, moreover, it had cheered us with a village band and laughing children on the green, but when their human sounds died out simultaneously with the disappearance of the sun behind the great shoulder of Calstock ridge, we shivered slightly.

But what were these strange ruins in the gloom? First a few deserted cottages, then a great broken stack, then rambling ruins of vaster and more mysterious form. We paddled now, through still water - silent, deep and opaquely green.

Building after building, broken, deserted, apparently abandoned in a hurry. It was a village, a veritable town. There was glass in the windows still, though mostly broken: there were doors ajar, just as if the occupants had gone out hastily in fear of some sudden catastrophe. But only the slow hand of decay had produced whatever changes had come about.

What made the place look still more accursed and desolate was the utter absence of vegetation. No grass had ventured to grow, though the town evidently was long ago abandoned. From where we sat in our boat, motionless with wonder, no grass or tree or shrub was to be seen. The mounded hills glowed with a baleful, coppery glare which turned blood-red where the sun caught the crests directly.

"Let us go back," said Jean in a whisper, but I demurred, for the place had fascinated me with its creepy mystery and I could not have turned back from prying into its secret for all the money in the world. I fastened *Sandpiper* to a big iron ring on one of the cracking quaysides, a ring that must have held much bigger boats in times gone by. Jean remained in *Sandpiper* watching for my reappearance apprehensively whenever I disappeared into buildings.

They were full of the strangest contrivances, nearly
rusted away, and beset with intricately designed pits
and cellars. Coming from one gloomy building I found
myself face to face with a huge mound, glowing a livid
blue-green in the dusk. From it came a steam, hard and
petrified now, gleaming a bright, harsh, unearthly
green. So that was the secret! I recognised this as a
compound of copper and arsenic. These were the copper
mines of Calstock's high noon, and the smelting had
separated from the copper this bitter poison which,
after seventy years, still held the countryside in a
death grip.

No sound broke the utter stillness or interrupted my
imagination in the task of repeopling this once busy
town, until Jean's voice echoed uncannily from the
serried ruins. I returned to find the olive-green,
sulky-looking river still sliding slowly inland like a
tired snake, and decided to venture further until definite signs of ebbing appeared. In this resolution we
were heartened by a fine spectacle ahead.

A great ridge rise very steeply from the river flats
to a height of five or six hundred feet. Though the
river and nearer hills had long sunk into a pool of
deep twilight, the fine cloak of woods draped over the
ridge was still lit with brilliant sunlight. It was a
sentinel in shining armour, guarding, as we were to
discover with joy, a valley of strangely beautiful
countryside.

I have no hesitation in saying that the scenery we
now came upon is probably the finest in Devon, com-
bining the Dart at its best with the grandeur of moorland dimensions and the subtle colouring of the limestone hills of Torbay. Yet it is unknown to tourists,
unnamed and unspoken among holidaymakers. For that
matter even residents are scarce. In another hour we
passed only one or two cottages - one a very lovely
golden colour and hidden far back in a jungle of rushes
- and a big old country house. Even these had an air
of wildness and complete isolation. Indeed, it is a
lost valley, separated from Plymouth and Tavistock by
the forbidding wastes of the copper fields, fenced from

Cornwall by the unbridged river, and walled off from the rest of Devon by the great ridge. Beyond the latter's sparkling crest, which rears itself up like nothing so much as an enormous, toppling ocean wave, lay all that other Devonshire which we knew and in which we were known: here we crept circumspectly like strangers in a strange land.

Now the river, which had lately become a cave of trees, turned westward into the faint afterglow of sunset and opened again into wide expanses of still bullrushes. But what were those queer shapes, as of twisted chimneys, darkly silhouetted against the sky? Once more we found ourselves in a land of ruins, but how extensive we could not tell. To judge by the enormous quayside, here overgrown with grass, it was as big as the other. But we had faced as much of these haunted hills as human nerves could stand in one night; and to clinch matters there issued from the dim quay above our heads a peal of weird, cacophonous laughter.

In the petrified silence which followed, the tide, with an audible sighing in the reeds, turned in its sleep: the bubbles and the green scum stirred seaward; we were permitted to return home.

Paddling downstream we were full of conjectures as to how far we had come and what this strange place might be, but we knew no names above Calstock. Actually it was labelled Morwellham, as we discovered on getting a map, later; but for us the mystery of what Morwellham might be waited solution for twelve months and that retreat in the night marked the end of our landward journey for the year.

With eyes straining in the gloom and ears attuned to catch each gurgle of the current on rock or bank, we picked our way down stream, hurrying past those haunted ruins. Once or twice, against the wan twilight lingering in the western sky, a gaunt ruin peered at us, or a tottering chimney lifted a threatening hand, but anon with relief we reached the more friendly lands by Calstock. We had scarcely breathed again when a piercing shriek rent the air and a fiery dragon roared across in an arc above our heads. A native of these parts might have been able to explain that it was the last train roaring across the lofty viaduct, but at the time, not knowing the viaduct was there, we felt our nerves were ruined for evermore.

We recognised the fact that we were at Calstock by one yellow lamp high up the hillside and through being bumped by the current against a leg of the viaduct. After that the night was jet black and the current in the gorges was such that frequently we didn't know in which direction we were trying to paddle. Indeed we gave up paddling and kept up our spirits by singing, doubtless to the mystification of lonely cottage dwellers on the banks.

There were no stars, no moon, no firm silhouettes of the wooded banks. We floated in a void, walled by blackness, moved by a mysteriously buoyant inky fluid, belonging to no land, situated neither in Devon nor Cornwall, hanging somewhere between heaven and earth.

Some of my friends say that I have the luck to have been born with a well-nigh infallible sense of direction, like that of homing birds, and it is certainly true that I have tried for years to lose myself – on moors and foggy seas and the by-ways of cities – to enjoy the experience of this sixth sense grappling with real difficulty; but in vain.

However, I can certainly get lost in print! I was about to relate how completely we were lost, being swept down the Tamar somewhere below Calstock. Jean was so oppressed by the blackness and sense of isolation that she lit the hurricane lamp and tied it to the mast. Vain effort: it succeeded only in making the blackness blacker, giving us the feeling of floating in the centre of a black velvet ball.

Then I had a complete conviction that if we strained our eyes hard enough over the port bow we should find ourselves opposite the silhouette of a domed hill. Sure enough we made out, ever so faintly, the familiar shape and, setting a course by it, presently came up to the over-hanging tree beneath our camp in the orchard creek.

Chapter 13

Plymouth and Journey's End

Though we dreamt of the beauty of that lost valley at whose portals we had stood and though the mystery of Morwellham often intrigued our minds, twelve months elapsed before we dropped over the high ridge to the creek where *Sandpiper* had been left as a hostage against our return.

Now we headed confidently upstream in broad daylight. Gone was the haunted, eerie atmosphere, but the beauty remained, transmuted into a bold and full-blown glory of summer. Morwellham at last appeared. We climbed on the tiled quays now grown high with grass and sat on bollards big enough to tether a liner, surveying a handful of cottages planted amidst the ruins of some vaster conception - mere shepherds' tents in the ruins of Pompeii. Not a soul moved, until in a weed-grown street, we came across a small boy with an imbecile expression who stared at us for thirty seconds as if he had never set eyes on human beings before, and vanished precipitately.

Incongruously among these ancient ruins stood a small modern hydro-electric station, an impressive concern of great pipes dropping from the ridge, of shining steel and delicate dials, seeming to be the handwork of an entirely different race from the ruin dwellers.

Still more canon country lay ahead. We passed by a limestone cliff honeycombed with caves and pinnacled with crags, altogether reminiscent of Dovedale in Derbyshire. Nor was the ensuing stretch, consisting of enormous hills, wooded luxuriantly with oaks, clustered masses of pine, maple, oak, birch, willow and elder, at all Devonshire in character. It reminded one unmistakably of the valleys of the Black Forest or the Upper Rhine, for the domesticated, park-like, miniature character of English scenery was lost. Strange, but fitting, that we should encounter practically at our journey's end the grandest scenery of all!

For *Sandpiper* was destined not to dip her prow into many more miles of untravelled water: that same evening we heard the roar of a weir and presently came in sight of the island and double waterfall at Weir Head.

Above Weir Head, so the villagers told us, the river passes through more mountainous scenery, through cleaves and gorges, past Gunnislake with its eight hundred foot test hill and Kit Hill sweeping up to a thousand feet, until it writhes in the throttling canons of Wareham Wood. Thereafter, in the ten-mile stretch by Launceston, it achieves a second lease of life, writhes no more and stretches itself comfortably across a broad green plain.

But *Sandpiper* was not to know those higher meadows. She had borne us from farthest north to Devon's farthest south. She had battled with the stony, icy rapids of the upper Dart and borne the torrid heat of Prawle. She had strained in fierce winds and fought stiff seas, currents and tides, all along the southern coast of Devon and had faithfully borne us into every mysterious creek and swift river. At Weir Head, with battered, leaking hull, with two broken ribs and with her wings of sail sadly tattered, she seemed to say that her journey was done. With her voyage of Devon's southern coast faithfully performed, she seemed to have but one wish; to run downstream with the tide - to sail the sea again by lovely Plymouth, a fitting last port, and to float to sleep perhaps a little way into the quiet Plym, home of ships whose days are done.

In the current that eddied below the weir island she swung her head downstream, and, granted her wish, she regained the blithe step of youth, heading swiftly southward. At Calstock we landed to offer first and last homage to Cornwall by eating Cornish cream, a somewhat thinner and inferior imitation of the Devonshire variety, and so by nightfall we landed at our old camp of the year before. Nothing had changed; not even the warm greeting of the old couple at the farm; for friendship perhaps means more in the country than in town.

I do not know how long we stayed, or how often we said 'to-morrow', but I remember that at last there came a day in which the strange stirring of wanderlust made itself felt in my bones - sure indication of autumn. Across the broad reed beds the swift clouds flung blue shadows and the feathery reeds whispered endlessly a song of autumn restlessness.

As we dropped down river we met a salt breeze from the sea, charged with a hint of tarry ropes from Devonport dockyards and of fading bracken on wave-beaten headlands. It came seeking us, forcing its way into the hills, taking from us the smell of mouldering woods, hedgerows and apple orchards, and our hearts leapt to it as readily as our little orange sail, which once more burned against a sky of purest blue.

The wind freshened as we swept past Pentillie Castle, on a swift seaward tide. But where Tamar leaves the hills, by Hole's Hole, and leaps on a straight run for the sea, the wind flung itself upon us with altogether too boisterous a welcome, until it created in the opposing tide steeply curled waves, ominously resembling those which had swamped us at Exmouth. A brilliant sun turned everything windward of us into molten, flowing gold. Heeling over perilously and fighting our way furlong by furlong, tacking perhaps a dozen times to the mile, we had unfortunately no occasion to appreciate the spectacle at leisure.

At the end of one Devonward tack we found waiting for us the same detestably sociable bull that we had met on our way upstream, and on the corresponding Cornish tack we nearly ran into a naval pinnace the coxswain of which so strikingly resembled the bull met at the other end of the tack, that Jean and I with difficulty prevented ourselves laughing at him openly - a piece of restraint for which we were shortly to congratulate ourselves.

For in ten minutes the wind blew amain, so that we heeled right over with sail quivering, and the pinnace came over to give us moral support. "Thank God we've got a Navy," I exclaimed, heaving my dripping sleeve out of the waves which raced along our coamings. But the big warships among which we now found ourselves rode this little storm without their giant sides giving a single tremor in sympathy with our tossing distress. They were as utterly unmoved as if they were great steel castles rooted in the rock, and I pondered on the almost limitless range of the sea which could set us dancing wildly to this shrill treble, but which, in its lower octaves, can make even these monstrous islands lurch and roll to founder helplessly.

Forcing our way between the Hoe and Drake's Island we found the wind had backed to east. It had long since blown the Sound clear of all sail boats, and even steamers laboured with stiff flags straining in the blast. Should we give up and be flung upon the coast of Cornwall? Never! We dropped the sail and paddled hard, with eyes set on the distant Plym and the haven of Oreston. Our paddles move through glue and our muscles ache as if they will snap. So bent are we on our own almost hopeless struggle that we fail to see the gigantic struggle of winds and clouds that is taking place out to sea - until a great crash of thunder makes us turn our heads and lift our eyes from the lashing rain squall, to behold in the west one great wall of blackness where ten minutes before was blue sky and bright cloud.

It is the old war of the kings of the east and the west winds - culminating in this desperate climax. For all too many days the north-easter has poured his sharp battalions into the kingdom of the south-west, until, misled by his easy victory, he has this morning broken into a furious charge. a headlong. reckless advance.

But the good-natured king of the west has awakened

from sleep. His rage rises. Ponderously his massed black chariots come up the Channel, darkening the sky, stabbing their way inexorably onward with lightning and the flash of chariot wheels. Against this threat the north-easter flings his reinforcements with one last howl of rage and desperation. The grey face of the Sound is whipped to streaky foam, whilst we gasp for breath and fight for the shelter of every rocky point along the Hoe, grimly winning foot by foot. Pray heaven the south-wester will come to our assistance before our muscles crack and our bodies fall limp under the cold lash of rain squalls and hours of ceaseless paddling.

Now the clouds are like heavy black hulls with billowing purple sails, making straight for Plymouth Sound, as if the battle is finally to be decided in that amphitheatre. Nearer and nearer comes the crash of the cannonade, brighter and brighter the lightning flashes, more and more weird the awesome light which hangs over Mount Edgecumbe and the Hoe.

Huddled from the wind and rain, people on the Hoe are watching the spectacle in awed wonder. Under the dark storm clouds a golden ray of sunlight has broken forth once more. It flashes on the towers and roofs of Plymouth, turns the masts and rigging of ships in Sutton Pool to a fine tracery of gold, and gilds the flying boats, swan-like on the bosom of the Plym. How we long to put into the old harbour! Since morning we have been battling against a head wind without a moment's pause to land or to eat, and now we have paddled for three hours gaining scarcely as many miles against the relentless wind and wave. My arms and back did not forget that ordeal for three weeks and my heart for much longer. But the Plym was definitely opening up before us, promising some green and quiet haven in which *Sandpiper* might settle at her journey's end.

The barbican is passed, that barbican built to replace the forts at the gateway to Sutton Pool. The old forts were erected by Henry VIII at the same time as the reinforcement of those at Dartmouth and were similarly connected by a great chain which closed the entrance at nightfall.

Surely the Plym should be a paradise for the modern artist! Docks, piers, chimney stacks and the old hulks that lie in dockyards, throw their gaunt grey patters against the loveliest and most softly-coloured countryside, beset with gently wooded hills and a few ancient

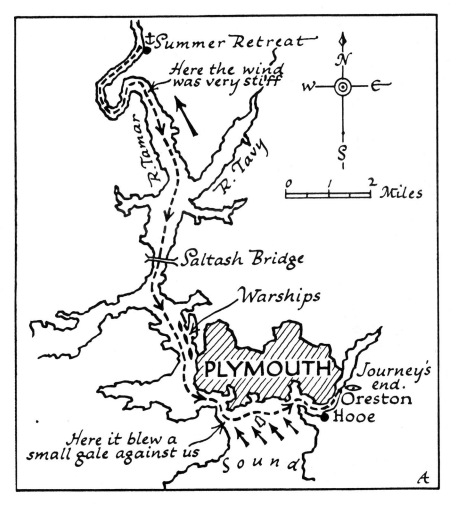

houses. At the head of the Plym is quiet, old-fashioned Plympton, aptly the home of one of England's greatest artists - Joshua Reynolds.

Opening up ahead and to starboard are the quaint

narrow village streets, the creeks and the basins of Oreston. The latter are big enough to hide the building of an armada but have held nothing these many years except the boats of local yachtsmen and a few old vessels in the dignity of abandonment. A queer and interesting region is this waterside of Hooe and Oreston. It is half country village, half abandoned dockyard. Here an unsophisticated green field runs down to the sea; there next to it is a bit of quayside which might be a slice of Limehouse docks.

Into the most quiet-looking of these creeks, just above the bridge by the Cattewater, *Sandpiper* turns her prow, but lingers as if she knew that this was the last glimpse she might ever take of the wide sea, the fair cities and that long coast, the richness of whose beauty has been endless.

The fierce wind has fallen at last; but the thunder pall gathers itself for one last rolling salute, hanging over the Plym as if to follow *Sandpiper* to her haven. With half-superstitious thought I recall that thunder baptised *Sandpiper* when first she met the sea and now thunder greets her as she homes from her longest flight.

At the end of the creek are a cluster of fishermen's cottages, some boats and yachts and an old mill. Behind them - incredible sound after so much sea and country - is the roar of a main road on which we may presently be borne in a few minutes into the pomp of Plymouth town. Already we have severed our thought from the sea. How often will the waters wait for the gentle breast of *Sandpiper* and the shadow of her wings? How many days of glorious light and freshening breeze will dawn on headland, river and sandy cove to find not a soul to enjoy them? Yet where *Sandpiper* cannot venture again, there may follow in the wake of her pilgrimage many other adventurers and seekers after beauty.

The storm is dissolving into a wide serenity of sunset, and Plymouth, silhouetted, greets us with the beacons of her gleaming, rain-washed spires. There is no other city at which our voyage could more fittingly terminate, for she is the queen city of Devon. Her sons and her visions have moulded the far corners of the earth. She has bequeathed her name to more daughter cities than has any other city in the world. From her lap have gone forth countless children to fight for desperate ventures and at her bidding expeditions have sailed out to encircle the globe. And whether her ships have returned treasure-laden and in the assured pride of conquest or with shattered rigging and heavy with broken hearts, she has folded them into the benediction of her queenly arms.

Possibly we are the tiniest sail of any that she has welcomed home, but she knows our cause has been a worthy one - to awaken the sentinels and rally the defenders of the unspoilt beauty of Devon - and she knows that we bring ashore a fabulous treasure - the stored memories of active, golden hours, sparkling with jewelled images of the incomparably lovely scenery of this fair county.

OTHER OBELISK PUBLICATIONS

AROUND & ABOUT THE HALDON HILLS, Chips Barber   £2.50

"... is worth every penny"   Exmouth Journal
"... certainly worth more than a fleeting glance"
Express & Echo, Exeter

THE LOST CITY OF EXETER, Chips Barber   £2.99

"... rich in historical background ... also packed with
lovely little anecdotes that have passed into local
folklore"   Western Morning News

DIARY OF A DARTMOOR WALKER, Chips Barber   £2.99

"It is a hilarious book"   Express & Echo
"It is for real walkers"   Exeter Flying Post

THE TORBAY BOOK, Chips Barber   £2.99

"Mr Barber's best yet"   Exmouth Journal
"Wonderfully nostalgic"   Herald Express, Torquay

AN EXETER BOYHOOD, Frank Retter   £2.50

"Highly Readable"   Exeter Flying Post
"Alive with characters and places" Western Morning News

ADVENTURE THROUGH RED DEVON, Raymond B Cattell   £2.99

"Immensely enjoyable"   Express & Echo
"An endearing Saga"   Devon Life

These titles are available from OBELISK PUBLICATIONS,
2 Church Hill, Pinhoe, Exeter. Postage free.